CANONGATE CLASSICS

An Anthology

Chosen and introduced by J. B. Pick

Foreword by Roderick Watson

Canongate Classics
1987–1997

First published by Canongate Books Ltd, 14 High Street,
Edinburgh, EH1 1TE. Selection and introductory notes copyright
© J. B. Pick 1997. Introduction © Roderick Watson 1997.

The publishers gratefully acknowledge general subsidy
from the Scottish Arts Council towards the Canongate
Classics Series.

Typeset by Hewer Text Composition Services, Edinburgh
Printed and bound in Great Britain by Caledonian
International, Bishopbriggs

British Library Cataloguing in Publication Data
A catalogue record is available on request from the
British Library

ISBN 0 86241 713 9

CONTENTS

Introduction Section	4	Clues to Fish	40
Clues to Seashore Animal		Identifying Coelenterates	44
types	10	Identifying Worms	48
Clues to Seashore Animal		Identifying Molluscs	52
eggs	18	Identifying Crustaceans	
Clues to Seashore Animal		and Insects	64
shells	22	Identifying Echinoderms	71
Clues to Seashore Animals		Identifying Fish	74
with jointed legs and shells	34	Index and Further Reading	80

ABOUT THIS BOOK

This book is about animals that live on the seashore. It allows you to identify the most common seashore animals of northern and western Europe and it also tells you a little about their lifestyles and habits.

The book is divided into three main sections: Introduction, Clues and Identification. The Introduction section tells you the best places and times to look for seashore animals, and how to catch them to study them in more detail. When you have looked at the living animals, be sure to put them back where you found them.

The Clues section allows you to identify each animal you have found. Start on page 10 and follow the clues. The arrows and numbers in the right-hand margin tell you which page to go to next.

The Identification Section consists of information about each major group of seashore animals and double-page colour plates illustrating the individual types or species. Most animals that you find will be illustrated in this section. Alongside each illustration is a basic description of the animal. Measurements are given in millimetres or centimetres – abbreviated to mm or cm (1 cm = 10 mm = 2/5th inch).

The coloured band at the top of each double-page spread helps you locate the relevant sections of the book: *blue* for Introduction, *yellow* for Clues, *red* for Identification. An arrowhead at the top right of a spread shows the topic continues on to the next spread. A bar at the top right indicates the end of that topic.

In order to use this book you will need real animals. They can be found in rock pools, under rocks and seaweed, and in the jetsam (things washed ashore).

The best time to hunt for animals on the seashore is when the tide is low. Start as near the sea as possible and keep a sharp lookout to see that the tide does not overtake you on either side.

Tides move in and out twice every twenty-four hours on most shores. When there is no moon or when the moon is full, tides are very high and very low. Watch the tides on your shore to find out:

How far the tides come up the shore; how far they go out.
How long the tide takes to cover the shore; how long it takes to go out.
What time of day the tides are very high.

EQUIPMENT – You will need polythene bags, plastic boxes and buckets for carrying the animals; a small net, a spade and a magnifying lens.

When you have looked at the living animals, put them back where you found them or keep them for a short time in aquariums filled with clean sea water.

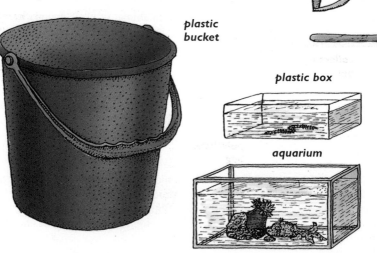

plastic bucket

plastic box

aquarium

Contents

Introduction   v

REEDOM
The Bruce, JOHN BARBOUR   1

The Pauper and the Pardoner
Ane Satyre of the Thrie Estaitis, SIR DAVID LINDSAY   2

Edom of Gordon
Scottish Ballads, ed. EMILY LYLE   8

Leaving Skye: Rough Seas
Journal of a Tour to the Hebrides, JAMES BOSWELL   13

The Glory and the Darkness
*The Private Memoirs and Confessions of a
Justified Sinner,* JAMES HOGG   18

The Pot and the Kettle
The Member, JOHN GALT   22

Plots and Deceptions
Memoirs of a Highland Lady, ELIZABETH GRANT   27

Stickeen and the Crevasse
Stickeen, JOHN MUIR   31

Taking a Wife
'The Beach of Falesá', ROBERT LOUIS STEVENSON   37

The Medal
The Exploits of Brigadier Gerard, ARTHUR CONAN
DOYLE   42

Wounded Feelings
The House with the Green Shutters, GEORGE DOUGLAS
BROWN   49

The Far Islands
The Watcher by the Threshold: Shorter Scottish Fiction,
JOHN BUCHAN   52

Topsail Janet and the Sea
Gillespie, J. MACDOUGALL HAY   55

Martha's Dance
The Quarry Wood, NAN SHEPHERD   61

Highland Mary
The Life of Robert Burns, CATHERINE CARSWELL   65

Taking Shelter
The Gowk Storm, NANCY BRYSSON MORRISON   70

A Leaf in the Wind
Sun Circle, NEIL M. GUNN   75

The Preacher and the Tinks
Cloud Howe, LEWIS GRASSIC GIBBON   79

Elizabeth and Elise
Imagined Corners, WILLA MUIR   83

In the Cellar
The Early Life of James McBey, JAMES MCBEY   86

The Gift of Courage
Private Angelo, ERIC LINKLATER   90

Kirstie's Funeral
Fergus Lamont, ROBIN JENKINS   94

'I do count them, Sean'
The People of the Sea, DAVID THOMSON   98

Ghosts
A Childhood in Scotland, CHRISTIAN MILLER   103

The Trap
Linmill Stories, ROBERT MCLELLAN   106

Hallaig
Modern Scottish Gaelic Poems, SORLEY MACLEAN   III

List of Canongate Classics   II7

Introduction

The idea of a Scottish 'classics' series began with a proposal from the Scottish Arts Council, inviting publishers to submit bids for a series which would establish a Scottish list and improve the production values of paperback reprints. Canongate won the contract ten years ago with a proposal which featured established classics in Scottish writing and also promised to develop our notions of what the 'classic' canon might be by publishing genres other than just fiction and poetry, by recognising women writers, and by bringing back to public attention hitherto forgotten or underrated titles. In keeping with the need for high quality paperbacks, the Canongate series was designed by George Mackie, and each volume was to be provided with an introduction and a brief summary of the author's life and work. None of this would have been possible without financial support from the Scottish Arts Council and, in the developing years, the personal commitment of Walter Cairns and Stephanie Wolfe Murray.

When a title is well-known or, indeed, already in print, the aim is to offset the best edition possible and accordingly a significant number of Canongate titles have been completely re-edited, with texts corrected, original matter restored, and notes, footnotes and glossaries specially provided whenever necessary. Highlights of this policy have been Rod Lyall's work on Lindsay's *Thrie Estaitis*, Andrew Tod's re-editing of the *Highland Lady* books, and Tom Crawford's definitive editions of Grassic Gibbon's *Scots Quair*. The series' most recent policy has been to develop the publication of omnibus editions with one volume containing several books, or with commissioned collections of, for example, the best writing from the Scottish Enlightenment. From the start a special commitment was made to Scottish women's writing: Willa Muir's *Imagined Corners* was Canongate Classic 1, while

Imagined Selves has collected much more of her writing and *The Grampian Quartet* has made available what amounts to the complete prose of Nan Shepherd.

Non-fiction can be found in the autobiographies of David Daiches, James McBey, Christian Miller, Catherine Carswell and Edwin Muir, and works of social, geographical and ecological interest feature equally clearly in John Muir's *Wilderness Journeys* as well as in books from Charles MacLean on St Kilda, Rebecca West on the Balkans, Janet Teissier du Cros on life in occupied France (her wonderful *Divided Loyalties* was crying out for a larger audience), and then there are David Thomson and F. Marian McNeill on folk lore and of course Boswell and Johnson on their famous tour of the Highlands. The Canongate Classics are still committed to high quality single editions, most notably a landmark new edition of Barbour's *The Bruce* and lesser-known titles such as Robert McLellan's *Linmill Stories*, or powerful novels from established modern writers such as Robin Jenkins and Neil Gunn. Indeed the Gunn books have introductions by John Pick and F.R. Hart, joint authors of the best critical biography of Gunn, and distinguished literary critics in their own right.

With over 80 titles published in the last ten years, the series has come a long way from the early days when Stephanie Wolfe Murray, John Pick, Tom Crawford and I first sat down to consider what a 'Scottish Classic' might be. Tom retired last year and the editorial team has been joined by Cairns Crag and Dorothy McMillan, but the question of 'classic' status remains as challenging and urgent as ever. If our aim can be summed-up, it is to provide the best available paperback editions of the most important books in the Scottish canon, to expand that canon by republishing hitherto 'forgotten' titles or authors, and finally to revalue and revitalise both these categories by placing them in fresh new combinations and contexts, as well as by providing authoritative scholarly and critical introductions. Perhaps the best test of this aim can be found in this anthology of passages from some of the Canongate Classics, specially chosen and introduced by John Pick to show something of the delights—and the surprises—still to be found in our literary tradition.

Roderick Watson (Series Editor)

To
Walter Cairns
and
Stephanie Wolfe Murray

[*Lines 225–242 are translated line for line*] (225) Ah! freedom is a noble thing/ Freedom lets a man have pleasure,/ Freedom all solace to man gives,/ He lives at ease who freely lives./ (229) A noble heart will have no ease/ Nor aught else that pleases him/ If freedom fails, for free decision/ Is longed for above all else./ No, he who has always lived free/ Cannot well know the properties,/ The anger, no, the miserable fate,/ That are coupled to foul thralldom./ (237) But, if he had experienced it/ Then he would know it perfectly/ And would think freedom more to be prized/ Than all the gold there is in this world./ (241) Thus opposites always are/ Revealing one about the other . . .

---

240. All the gold. Barbour probably recalled the moral added by Walter the Englishman, archbishop of Palermo at the end of the twelfth century to his translation of Phaedrus' version of the fable of the wolf and the dog: 'I am not in such need that I should want to make myself a serf for the sake of my belly . . . The serf does not own himself or his property, whereas a free man does. Freedom, the eminently sweet good, contains all other goods . . . Freedom cannot be sold for all the gold in existence, this heavenly good excels earthly wealth.'

JOHN BARBOUR

Freedom
from THE BRUCE

JOHN BARBOUR (1320–95) regarded his epic of Robert
Bruce as at once chronicle and romance; the poem is a
hero-tale, related with straightforward clarity and force.
Barbour himself was no warrior, but a Churchman who
became Archdeacon of Aberdeen, and later an auditor
of the exchequer for King Robert II.

[*In praise of freedom; on the pains of thralldom*]

225   A! Fredome is a noble thing
      Fredome mays man to haiff liking.
      Fredome all solace to man giffis,
      He levys at es that frely levys.
      A noble hart may haiff nane es
230   Na ellys nocht that may him ples
      Gyff fredome failyhe, for fre liking
      Is yharnyt our all other thing.
      Na he that ay has levyt fre
      May nocht knaw weill the propyrté
235   The angyr na the wrechyt dome
      That is couplyt to foule thyrldome,
      Bot gyff he had assayit it.
      Than all perquer he suld it wyt,
      And suld think fredome mar to prys
240   Than all the gold in warld that is.
      Thus contrar thingis evermar
      Discoveryngis off the tother ar . . .

[from *The Bruce*, Book I, pp. 48–51]

The Pauper and the Pardoner

from ANE SATYRE OF THE THRIE ESTAITIS

An influential courtier, SIR DAVID LINDSAY OF THE MOUNT (1490–1555) was usher to the infant prince after the death of James IV at Flodden, and later Lyon King of Arms, on several occasions serving as ambassador abroad, where he may have encountered the writings of Reformers.

His attack on the Church in *The Thrie Estaitis*, however, is concerned with conduct rather than with doctrine, and strikes home today as a denunciation of the corruptions of power.

In this extract the exploitation of a poor man by the venal peddler of indulgences is central to the moral drive of the play.

DILIGENCE

1965   Quhat Devill ails this cruckit carle?

PAUPER

                      Marie, meikill sorrow;

I can not get, thocht I gasp, to beg nor to borrow.

DILIGENCE

Quhair, devill, is this thou dwels; or quhats thy intent?

PAUPER

1970   I dwell into Lawthiane, ane myle fra Tranent.

DILIGENCE

Quhair wald thou be, carle, the suth to me schaw?

PAUPER

Sir, evin to Sanct Androes, for to seik law.

DILIGENCE

For to seik law, in Edinburgh was the neirest way.

PAUPER

Sir, I socht law thair this monie deir day,

2

1975 Bot I culd get nane at Sessioun nor Seinye:
Thairfoir the mekill dum Devill droun all the meinye!

DILIGENCE

Shaw me thy mater, man, with al the circumstances,
How that thou hes happinit on thir unhappie
chances.

PAUPER

Gude-man, will ye gif me your charitie,
1980 And I sall declair yow the black veritie.
My father was ane auld man and ane hoir,
And was of age fourscoir of yeirs and moir,
And Mald, my mother, was fourscoir and fyfteine;
And with my labour I did thame baith susteine.
1985 Wee had ane meir that caryit salt and coill,
And everie ilk yeir scho brocht us hame ane foill.
Wee had thrie ky that was baith fat and fair,
Nane tydier [hyne to] the toun of Air.
My father was sa waik of blude and bane
That he deit, quhairfoir my mother maid great maine;
1990 Then scho deit, within ane day or two,
And thair began my povertie and wo.
Our gude gray meir was baittand on the feild,
And our lands laird tuik hir for his hyreild.
The Vickar tuik the best cow be the head
1995 Incontinent, quhen my father was deid;
And quhen the Vickar hard tel how that my mother
Was dead, fra-hand he tuke to him ane uther.
Then Meg, my wife, did murne both evin and morow,
Till at the last scho deit for verie sorow;
2000 And quhen the Vickar hard tell my wyfe was dead,
The thrid cow he cleikit be the head.
Thair umest clayis, that was of rapploch gray,

Sessioun *the Court of Session, the supreme secular court*
Seinye *Consistory Court* meinye *company* hoir *grey-
haired* ky *cattle* tydier *rich in milk* hyne *from here*
baittand *grazing* hyreild *heriot, the mortuary due owed to the
lord* umest clayis *upper garments, along with the corspresent or
'cow' mortuary dues owed to the vicar* rapploch *homespun*

The Vickar gart his clark bear them away.
Quhen all was gaine, I micht mak na debeat
2005 Bot with all my bairns past for till beg my meat.
Now have I tald yow the blak veritie,
How I am brocht into this miserie.

DILIGENCE

How did the person? Was he not thy gude freind?

PAUPER

The Devil stick him, he curst me for my teind,
2010 And halds me yit under that same proces,
That gart me want the Sacrament at Pasche.
In gude faith, Sir, thocht [ye] wald cut my throt,
I have na geir except ane Inglis grot,
Quhilk I purpois to gif ane man of law.

DILIGENCE

2015 Thou art the daftest fuill that ever I saw!
Trows thou, man, be the law to get remeid
Of men of kirk? Na, nocht till thou be deid!

PAUPER

Sir, be quhat law, tell me, quhairfoir or quhy
That ane Vickar sould tak fra me thrie ky?

DILIGENCE

2020 Thay have na law, exceptand consuetude,
Quhilk law to them is sufficient and gude.

PAUPER

Ane consuetude against the common weill
Sould be na law, I think, be sweit Sanct Geill!
Quhair will ye find that law, tell gif ye can,
2025 To tak thrie ky fra ane pure husband-man?
Ane for my father, and for my wife ane uther,
And the thrid cow he tuke [for] Mald my mother.

DILIGENCE

It is thair law, all that thay have in use,
Thocht it be cow, sow, ganer, gryse or guse.

---

teind *tithe* Pasche *Easter* geir *property* Inglis grot *an
English coin, worth four pence* consuetude *custom* ganer
gander gryse *suckling pig*

PAUPER

2030   Sir, I wald speir at yow ane questioun:
Behauld sum prelats of this regioun,
Manifestlie during thair lustie lyfis
Thay swyfe ladies, madinis and uther men[ni]s wyfis,
And sa thair cunts thay have in consuetude!
2035   Quhidder say ye that law is evill or gude?

    DILIGENCE

Hald thy toung, man, it seims that thou war mangit!
Speik thou of preists, but doubt thou will be hangit.

    PAUPER

Be Him that bure the cruell croun of thorne,
I cair nocht to be hangit, evin the morne!

    DILIGENCE

2040   Be sure of preistis thou will get na support.

    PAUPER

Gif that be trew, the Feind resave the sort!
Sa, sen I se I get na uther grace,
I will ly doun and rest mee in this place.

Pauper lyis doun in the feild. Pardoner enters.

. . .

    PAUPER

Quhat thing was yon that I hard crak and cry?
I have bene dreamand and dreveland of my ky.
With my richt hand my haill bodie I saine:
2230   Sanct Bryd, Sanct Bryd, send me my ky againe!
I se standand yonder ane halie man;
To mak me help let me se gif he can.
Halie maister, God speid yow and gude morne!

    PARDONER

Welcum to me, thocht thou war at the horne!
2235   Cum, win the pardoun, and syne I sall the saine.

    PAUPER

Wil that pardoun get me my ky againe?

———

dreveland *raving*   **saine** *bless, cross*

PARDONER

Carle, of thy ky I have nathing ado;
Cum, win my pardon, and kis my relicts to.
Heir sall he saine him with his relictis.
Now lows thy pursse and lay doun thy offrand,

2240   And thou sall have my pardon evin fra-hand.
With raipis and relicts I sall the saine againe;
Of gut or gravell thou sall never have paine.
Now win the pardon, limmer, or thou art lost!

PAUPER

My haly father, quhat will that pardon cost?

PARDONER

2245   Let me quhat mony thou bearest in thy bag.

PAUPER

I have ane grot heir, bund into a rag.

PARDONER

Hes thou na uther silver bot ane groat?

PAUPER

Gif I have mair, sir, cum and rype my coat!

PARDONER

Gif me that grot, man, gif thou hest na mair.

PAUPER

2250   With all my heart, maister: lo, tak it thair.
Now let me se your pardon, with your leif.

PARDONER

Ane thousand yeir of pardons I the geif.

PAUPER

Ane thousand yeir? I will not live sa lang!
Delyver me it, maister, and let me gang.

PARDONER

2255   Ane thousand yeir I lay upon thy head,
With *totiens quotiens* now mak me na mair plead!
Thou hast resaifit thy pardon now already.

PAUPER

Bot I can se na thing, sir, be our [Leddy]!
Forsuith, maister, I trow I be not wyse

———

gravell *kidney stones*
totiens quotiens '*as often as . . . so often*'

2260   To pay ere I have sene my marchandryse.
That ye have gottin my groat full sair I rew!
Sir, quhidder is your pardon black or blew?
Maister, sen ye have taine fra me my cunyie,
My marchandryse schaw me, withouttin sunyie,
2265   Or to the Bischop I sall pas and pleinyie
In Sanct Androis, and summond yow to the Seinyie.

     PARDONER

Quhat craifis the, carle? Me thinks thou art not wise!

     PAUPER

I craif my groat, or ellis my marchandrise.

     PARDONER

I gaif the pardon for ane thowsand yeir.

     PAUPER

2270   How shall I get that pardon, let me heir.

     PARDONER

Stand still and I sall tell [the] the haill storie:
Quhen thow art deid and gais to Purgatorie,
Being condempit to paine a thowsand yeir,
Then sall thy pardoun the releif, but weir.
2275   Now be content. Ye ar ane mervalous man!

     PAUPER

Sall I get nathing for my grot quhill than?

     PARDONER

That sall thou not, I mak it to yow plaine.

     PAUPER

Na? Than, gossop, gif me my grot againe!

[from *Ane Satyre of the Thrie Estaitis*, pp. 71–3, 80–2]

Edom of Gordon

from SCOTTISH BALLADS

The Scottish Ballads were composed to be sung, and have come down to us as orally transmitted poems. The three verses which drive home the feelings of the raider as he gazes down at the girl he has killed are among the strangest and strongest in the entire tradition.

1 It fell about the Martinmas,
   When the wind blew schrile and cauld,
Said Edom o Gordon to his men,
   We maun draw to a hald.

2 'And what an a hald sall we draw to,
   My merry men and me?
We will gae to the house of the Rhodes,
   To see that fair lady.'

3 She had nae sooner busket her sell,
   Nor putten on her gown,
Till Edom o Gordon and his men
   Were round about the town.

4 They had nae sooner sitten down,
   Nor sooner said the grace,
Till Edom o Gordon and his men
   Were closed about the place.

1 Martinmas 11*th of November* schrile *biting*   draw to a
hald   *head for a place of shelter*
2 what an a *which particular*
3 busket *dressed* town *settlement*

8

5 The lady ran up to her tower-head,
    As fast as she could drie,
To see if by her fair speeches
    She could with him agree.

6 As soon as he saw the lady fair,
    And hir yates all locked fast,
He fell into a rage of wrath,
    And his heart was aghast.

7 'Cum down to me, ye lady fair,
    Cum down to me; let's see;
This night ye's ly by my ain side,
    The morn my bride sall be.'

8 'I winnae cum down, ye fals Gordon,
    I winnae cum down to thee,
I winnae forsake my ane dear lord,
    That is sae far frae me.'

9 'Gi up your house, ye fair lady,
    Gi up your house to me,
Or I will burn yoursel therein,
    Bot and your babies three.'

10 'I winnae gie up, you fals Gordon,
    To nae sik traitor as thee,
Tho you should burn mysel therein,
    Bot and my babies three.'

11 'Set fire to the house,' quoth fals Gordon,
    'Sin better may nae bee;
And I will burn hersel therein,
    Bot and her babies three.'

5 drie *do*
7 the morn *tomorrow*
9 bot and *and also*

12 'And ein wae worth ye, Jock my man!
    I paid ye weil your fee;
Why pow ye out my ground-wa-stane,
    Lets in the reek to me?

13 'And ein wae worth ye, Jock my man!
    For I paid you weil your hire;
Why pow ye out my ground-wa-stane,
    To me lets in the fire?'

14 'Ye paid me weil my hire, lady,
    Ye paid me weil my fee,
But now I'm Edom of Gordon's man,
    Maun either do or die.'

15 O then bespake her youngest son,
    Sat on the nurse's knee,
'Dear mother, gie owre your house,' he says,
    'For the reek it worries me.'

16 'I winnae gie up my house, my dear,
    To nae sik traitor as he;
Cum weil, cum wae, my jewels fair,
    Ye maun tak share wi me.'

17 'O then bespake her dochter dear,
    She was baith jimp and sma;
'O row me in a pair o shiets,
    And tow me owre the wa.'

18 They rowd her in a pair of shiets,
    And towd her owre the wa,
But on the point of Edom's speir
    She gat a deadly fa.

12 ein *even* wae worth ye *may sorrow come to
you* pow *pull* ground-wa-stane *stone at
ground level* reek *smoke*
14 fee *wages*
15 gie owre *surrender* worries *chokes*
17 bespake *spoke* jimp *slender* row *wrap*
tow me *lower me by rope*

19 O bonny, bonny was hir mouth,
    And chirry were her cheiks,
  And clear, clear was hir yellow hair,
    Whereon the reid bluid dreips!

20 Then wi his speir he turnd hir owr;
    O gin hir face was wan!
  He said, You are the first that eer
    I wist alive again.

21 He turned hir owr and owr again;
    O gin hir skin was whyte!
  He said, I might ha spard thy life
    To been some mans delyte.

22 'Busk and boon, my merry men all,
    For ill dooms I do guess;
  I cannae luik in that bonny face,
    As it lyes on the grass.'

23 'Them luiks to freits my master deir,
    Then freits will follow them;
  Let it neir be said brave Edom o Gordon
    Was daunted with a dame.'

24 O then he spied hir ain deir lord,
    As he came owr the lee;
  He saw his castle in a fire,
    As far as he could see.

25 'Put on, put on, my mighty men,
    As fast as ye can drie!
  For he that's hindmost of my men
    Sall neir get guid o me.'

20 gin *how* wist *wished*
22 busk and boon *make ready* dooms *judgement*
23 them luiks to freits *those who regard omens*
24 lee *grass land*
25 put on *press on* drie *manage*

26 And some they raid, and some they ran,
   Fu fast out-owr the plain,
But lang, lang eer he could get up
   They were a' deid and slain.

27 But mony were the mudie men
   Lay gasping on the grien;
For o fifty men that Edom brought out
   There were but five ged heme.

28 And mony were the mudie men
   Lay gasping on the grien,
And mony were the fir ladys
   Lay lemanless at heme.

29 And round and round the waes he went,
   Their ashes for to view;
At last into the flames he flew,
   And bad the world adieu.

[from *Scottish Ballads*, pp. 55–9]

26 out-owr *over*
27 mudie *bold*
28 lemanless *without lovers*
29 waes *walls*

JAMES BOSWELL

Leaving Skye: Rough Seas
from JOURNAL OF A TOUR TO THE HEBRIDES

JAMES BOSWELL (1740–95) persuaded his friend and
mentor, the thoroughly urban Dr Johnson, to tour
Scotland in 1773, a trip which produced Johnson's
A Journey to the Western Islands and Boswell's own
Journal of a Tour to the Hebrides. This account of a
stormy passage has its ironies, with Boswell proudly
and fearfully stumping the deck, while Johnson lay
cosily asleep below.

While we were chatting in the indolent stile of men who
were to stay here all this day at least, we were suddenly
roused by being told that the wind was fair, that a little
fleet of herring-busses was passing by for Mull, and that
Mr. Simpson's vessel was about to sail. Hugh M'Donald,
the skipper, came to us, and was impatient that we should
get ready, which we soon did. Dr. Johnson, with composure
and solemnity, repeated the observation of Epictetus, that,
'as man has the voyage of death before him,—whatever may
be his employment, he should be ready at the master's call;
and an old man should never be far from the shore, lest he
should not be able to get himself ready.' He rode, and I
and the other gentlemen walked, about an English mile to
the shore, where the vessel lay. Dr. Johnson said, he should
never forget Sky, and returned thanks for all civilities. We
were carried to the vessel in a small boat which she had,
and we set sail very briskly about one o'clock. I was much
pleased with the motion for many hours. Dr. Johnson grew
sick, and retired under cover, as it rained a good deal.
I kept above, that I might have fresh air, and finding
myself not affected by the motion of the vessel, I exulted
in being a stout seaman, while Dr. Johnson was quite in a
state of annihilation. But I was soon humbled; for after
imagining that I could go with ease to America or the

East-Indies, I became very sick, but kept above board, though it rained hard.

As we had been detained so long in Sky by bad weather, we gave up the scheme that Col had planned for us of visiting several islands, and contented ourselves with the prospect of seeing Mull, and Icolmkill and Inchkenneth, which lie near to it.

Mr. Simpson was sanguine in his hopes for a while, the wind being fair for us. He said, he would land us at Icolmkill that night. But when the wind failed, it was resolved we should make for the sound of Mull, and land in the harbour of Tobermorie. We kept near the five herring vessels for some time; but afterwards four of them got before us, and one little wherry fell behind us. When we got in full view of the point of Ardnamurchan, the wind changed, and was directly against our getting into the sound. We were then obliged to tack, and get forward in that tedious manner. As we advanced, the storm grew greater, and the sea very rough. Col then began to talk of making for Egg, or Canna, or his own island. Our skipper said, he would get us into the Sound. Having struggled for this a good while in vain, he said, he would push forward till we were near the land of Mull, where we might cast anchor, and lie till the morning; for although, before this, there had been a good moon, and I had pretty distinctly seen not only the land of Mull, but up the Sound, and the country of Morven as at one end of it, the night was now grown very dark. Our crew consisted of one M'Donald, our skipper, and two sailors, one of whom had but one eye; Mr. Simpson himself, Col, and Hugh M'Donald his servant, all helped. Simpson said, he would willingly go for Col, if young Col or his servant would undertake to pilot us to a harbour; but, as the island is low land, it was dangerous to run upon it in the dark. Col and his servant appeared a little dubious. The scheme of running for Canna seemed then to be embraced; but Canna was ten leagues off, all out of our way; and they were afraid to attempt the harbour of Egg. All these different plans were successively in agitation. The old skipper still tried to make for the land of Mull; but then it was considered that there was no place there where we could anchor in safety.

Much time was lost in striving against the storm. At last it became so rough, and threatened to be so much worse, that Col and his servant took more courage, and said they would undertake to hit one of the harbours in Col.—'Then let us run for it in GOD's name,' said the skipper; and instantly we turned towards it. The little wherry which had fallen behind us, had hard work. The master begged that, if we made for Col, we should put out a light to him. Accordingly one of the sailors waved a glowing peat for some time. The various difficulties that were started, gave me a good deal of apprehension, from which I was relieved, when I found we were to run for a harbour before the wind. But my relief was but of short duration; for I soon heard that our sails were very bad, and were in danger of being torn in pieces, in which case we should be driven upon the rocky shore of Col. It was very dark, and there was a heavy and incessant rain. The sparks of the burning peat flew so much about, that I dreaded the vessel might take fire. Then, as Col was a sportsman, and had powder on board, I figured that we might be blown up. Simpson and he appeared a little frightened, which made me more so; and the perpetual talking, or rather shouting, which was carried on in Erse, alarmed me still more. A man is always suspicious of what is saying in an unknown tongue; and, if fear be his passion at the time, he grows more afraid. Our vessel often lay so much on one side, that I trembled lest she should be overset; and indeed they told me afterwards, that they had run her sometimes to within an inch of the water, so anxious were they to make what haste they could before the night should be worse. I now saw what I never saw before, a prodigious sea, with immense billows coming upon a vessel, so as that it seemed hardly possible to escape. There was something grandly horrible in the sight. I am glad I have seen it once. Amidst all these terrifying circumstances, I endeavoured to compose my mind. It was not easy to do it; for all the stories that I had heard of the dangerous sailing among the Hebrides, which is proverbial, came full upon my recollection. When I thought of those who were dearest to me, and would suffer severely, should I be lost, I upbraided myself, as not having a sufficient cause for putting myself in such danger. Piety afforded me comfort; yet I was disturbed by the objections that have been made against a particular providence, and by the arguments of those who maintain that it is in vain to hope that the petitions of an individual, or even of congregations, can have any influence with the Deity; objections which have been often made, and which Dr. Hawkesworth has lately revived, in his Preface to the Voyages to the South Seas; but Dr. Ogden's excellent doctrine on the efficacy of intercession prevailed.

It was half an hour after eleven before we set ourselves in the course for Col. As I saw them all busy doing something, I asked Col, with much earnestness, what I could do. He, with a happy readiness, put into my hand a rope, which was fixed to the top of one of the masts, and told me to hold it till he bade me pull. If I had considered the matter, I might have seen that this could not be of the least service; but his object was to keep me out of the way of those who were busy working the vessel, and at the same time to divert my fear, by employing me, and making me think that I was of use. Thus did I stand firm to my post, while the wind and rain beat upon me, always expecting a call to pull my rope.

The man with one eye steered; old M'Donald, and Col and his servant, lay upon the fore-castle, looking sharp out for the harbour. It was necessary to carry much *cloth*, as they termed it, that is to say, much sail, in order to keep the vessel off the shore of Col. This made violent plunging in a rough sea. At last they spied the harbour of Lochiern, and Col cried, 'Thank GOD, we are safe!' We ran up till we were opposite to it, and soon afterwards we got into it, and cast anchor.

Dr. Johnson had all this time been quiet and unconcerned. He had lain down on one of the beds, and having got free from sickness, was satisfied. The truth is, he knew nothing of the danger we were in: but, fearless and unconcerned, might have said, in the words which he has chosen for the motto to his *Rambler*,

Quo me cunque rapit tempestas, deferor hospes.[1]

Once, during the doubtful consultations, he asked whither we were going; and upon being told that it was not certain

---

1. For as the tempest drives, I shape my way. FRANCIS.

whether to Mull or Col, he cried, 'Col for my money!'—I now went down, with Col and Mr. Simpson, to visit him. He was lying in philosophick tranquillity, with a greyhound of Col's at his back, keeping him warm. Col is quite the *Juvenis qui gaudet canibus.* He had, when we left Talisker, two greyhounds, two terriers, a pointer, and a large Newfoundland water-dog. He lost one of his terriers by the road, but had still five dogs with him. I was very ill, and very desirous to get to shore. When I was told that we could not land that night, as the storm had now increased, I looked so miserably, as Col afterwards informed me, that what Shakspeare has made the Frenchman say of the English soldiers, when scantily dieted, '*Piteous they will look, like drowned mice!*' might, I believe, have been well applied to me. There was in the harbour, before us, a Campbell-town vessel, the Betty, Kenneth Morison master, taking in kelp, and bound for Ireland. We sent our boat to beg beds for two gentlemen, and that the master would send his boat, which was larger than ours. He accordingly did so, and Col and I were accommodated in his vessel till the morning.

[from *Journal of a Tour to the Hebrides* in the Canongate Classics omnibus edition, *Journey to the Hebrides*, pp. 372–6]

JAMES HOGG

The Glory and the Darkness

from CONFESSIONS OF A JUSTIFIED SINNER

JAMES HOGG (1770–1835) was a self-educated writer of
great subtlety and strength, who was grossly underesti-
mated in his day. Brought up in the Borders and steeped
in local lore, Hogg had a depth of vision which was
not mere fantasy. *The Private Memoirs and Confessions of
a Justified Sinner* is now recognised as the most powerful
and influential novel in a peculiarly Scottish metaphysical
tradition. His other works, often extravagant and variable,
show real imaginative force, and deserve the attention they
have begun to receive.

George was, from infancy, of stirring active disposition, and
could not endure confinement; and, having been of late
much restrained in his youthful exercises by this singular
persecutor, he grew uneasy under such restraint, and, one
morning, chancing to awaken very early, he arose to make an
excursion to the top of Arthur's Seat, to breathe the breeze of
the dawning, and see the sun arise out of the eastern ocean.
The morning was calm and serene; and as he walked down
the south back of the Canongate, toward the Palace, the
haze was so close around him that he could not see
the houses on the opposite side of the way. As he passed the
lord-commissioner's house, the guards were in attendance,
who cautioned him not to go by the Palace, as all the gates
would be shut and guarded for an hour to come, on which
he went by the back of St Anthony's gardens, and found his
way into that little romantic glade adjoining to the Saint's
chapel and well. He was still involved in a blue haze, like a
dense smoke, but yet in the midst of it the respiration was
the most refreshing and delicious. The grass and the flowers
were laden with dew; and, on taking off his hat to wipe his
forehead, he perceived that the black glossy fur of which his
chaperon was wrought, was all covered with a tissue of the

18

most delicate silver—a fairy web, composed of little spheres, so minute that no eye could discern any one of them; yet there they were shining in lovely millions. Afraid of defacing so beautiful and so delicate a garnish, he replaced his hat with the greatest caution, and went on his way light of heart.

As he approached the swire at the head of the dell,—that little delightful verge from which in one moment the eastern limits and shores of Lothian arise on the view,—as he approached it, I say, and a little space from the height, he beheld, to his astonishment, a bright halo in the cloud of haze, that rose in a semi-circle over his head like a pale rainbow. He was struck motionless at the view of the lovely vision; for it so chanced that he had never seen the same appearance before, though common at early morn. But he soon perceived the cause of the phenomenon, and that it proceeded from the rays of the sun from a pure unclouded morning sky striking upon this dense vapour which refracted them. But the better all the works of nature are understood, the more they will be ever admired. That was a scene that would have entranced the man of science with delight, but which the uninitiated and sordid man would have regarded less than the mole rearing up his hill in silence and in darkness.

George did admire this halo of glory, which still grew wider, and less defined, as he approached the surface of the cloud. But, to his utter amazement and supreme delight, he found, on reaching the top of Arthur's Seat, that this sublunary rainbow, this terrestrial glory, was spread in its most vivid hues beneath his feet. Still he could not perceive the body of the sun, although the light behind him was dazzling; but the cloud of haze lying dense in that deep dell that separates the hill from the rocks of Salisbury, and the dull shadow of the hill mingling with that cloud, made the dell a pit of darkness. On that shadowy cloud was the lovely rainbow formed, spreading itself on a horizontal plain, and having a slight and brilliant shade of all the colours of the heavenly bow, but all of them paler and less defined. But this terrestrial phenomenon of the early morn cannot be better delineated than by the name given of it by the shepherd boys, 'The little wee ghost of the rainbow.'

Such was the description of the morning, and the wild shades of the hill, that George gave to his father and Mr Adam Gordon that same day on which he had witnessed them; and it is necessary that the reader should comprehend something of their nature, to understand what follows.

He seated himself on the pinnacle of the rocky precipice, a little within the top of the hill to the westward, and, with a light and buoyant heart, viewed the beauties of the morning and inhaled its salubrious breeze. 'Here,' thought he, 'I can converse with nature without disturbance, and without being intruded on by any appalling or obnoxious visitor.' The idea of his brother's dark and malevolent looks coming at that moment across his mind, he turned his eyes instinctively to the right, to the point where that unwelcome guest was wont to make his appearance. Gracious Heaven! What an apparition was there presented to his view! He saw, delineated in the cloud, the shoulders, arms, and features of a human being of the most dreadful aspect. The face was the face of his brother, but dilated to twenty times the natural size. Its dark eyes gleamed on him through the mist, while every furrow of its hideous brow frowned deep as the ravines on the brow of the hill. George started, and his hair stood up in bristles as he gazed on this horrible monster. He saw every feature, and every line of the face, distinctly, as it gazed on him with an intensity that was hardly brookable. Its eyes were fixed on him, in the same manner as those of some carnivorous animal fixed on its prey; and yet there was fear and trembling, in these unearthly features, as plainly depicted as murderous malice. The giant apparition seemed sometimes to be cowering down as in terror, so that nothing but its brow and eyes were seen; still these never turned one moment from their object—again it rose imperceptibly up, and began to approach with great caution; and as it neared, the dimensions of its form lessened, still continuing, however, far above the natural size.

George conceived it to be a spirit. He could conceive it to be nothing else; and he took it for some horrid demon by which he was haunted, that had assumed the features of his brother in every lineament, but in taking on itself the human form, had miscalculated dreadfully on the size, and presented itself thus to him in a blown-up, dilated frame of embodied air, exhaled from the caverns of death or the regions of devouring fire. He was farther confirmed in the belief that it was a malignant spirit, on perceiving that it approached him across the front of a precipice, where there was not footing for things of mortal frame. Still, what with terror and astonishment, he continued rivetted to the spot, till it approached, as he deemed, to within two yards of him; and then, perceiving that it was setting itself to make a violent spring on him, he started to his feet and fled distractedly in the opposite direction, keeping his eye cast behind him lest he had been seized in that dangerous place. But the very first bolt that he made in his flight he came in contact with a *real* body of flesh and blood, and that with such violence that both went down among some scragged rocks, and George rolled over the other. The being called out 'Murder;' and, rising, fled precipitately. George then perceived that it was his brother; and, being confounded between the shadow and the substance, he knew not what he was doing or what he had done; and there being only one natural way of retreat from the brink of the rock, he likewise arose and pursued the affrighted culprit with all his speed towards the top of the hill. Wringhim was braying out 'Murder! murder!' at which George being disgusted, and his spirits all in a ferment from some hurried idea of intended harm, the moment he came up with the craven he seized him rudely by the shoulder, and clapped his hand on his mouth. 'Murder, you beast!' said he; 'what do you mean by roaring out murder in that way? Who the devil is murdering you, or offering to murder you?'

[from *The Private Memoirs and Confessions of a Justified Sinner*, pp. 32–5)

JOHN GALT

The Pot and the Kettle

from THE MEMBER

JOHN GALT (1779–1839), born in Ayrshire, and a dabbler
in a variety of business enterprises at home and abroad,
chose to see literature as a sideline, but his books are proof
that writing was his vocation. The novels are unusually
diverse and realistic for the time and place, and their
humour cuts close to the bone.

The Member in the book of that name spends his time
sliding, ducking, and dodging to retain independence of
political parties and privileged personages; the chapter
extracted here shows him interrogating a fellow politician
accused of indulging in precisely the dubious stratagems
he employed himself a few chapters earlier.

Although the first session of my third parliament worked
on myself a considerable change, and led me on to be more
of a public and party man than was in exact conformity
with my own notions of what a plain member should be,
who has the real good of his country at heart, I yet had
some small business in my own particular line; the most
remarkable piece of which was in being balloted a member
of a committee to try the election for the borough of Wordam,
in which it was said that some of the most abominable bribery
practices had taken place that ever offended the sight of the
sun at noon-day. In this affair my old adversary at Frailtown,
Mr. Gabblon, was the sitting member; and to be sure the
petitioners alleged against him such things as might have
made the hair on the Speaker's wig stand on end 'like
quills upon the fretful porcupine,' had they not been so
well accustomed to accusations of the same kind.

It is true that there are few tribunals more pure and
impartial than the election committees of the House of
Commons; but incidents will occur in the course of an
inquiry that are very apt to make the proceedings seem

22

questionable; and thus it came to pass, that as we reported Mr. Gabblon not duly elected, I suffered in the opinion of his friends, as having been swayed by the recollection of the trouble he had given me at Frailtown. No man, however, could act with stricter justice than I did: one of the committee, indeed, a new young member, fresh from Oxford, and aspiring for renown, said openly, that I had shewn a conduct throughout the investigation worthy of Rhadamanthus; which nick-name, by the by, did not stick to me, but to himself.

Among other charges, it was alleged against Mr. Gabblon that he had hired a mountebank doctor and a merry-andrew to seduce the burgesses; I pricked up my ears at this, and looking from under my brows, and over the table to where the honourable gentleman was sitting, gave him, in spite of myself, a most, as he called it, taunting smile. Now, the truth was, that I only happened to call to mind what Mr. Tough, my solicitor, had done with Doctor Muckledose at the Frailtown election.

The mention of the mountebank did not, however, make a deep impression on the committee; indeed, some of themselves, if all tales be true, were well accustomed to such antics; but an answer to a very small question, which I put to one of the witnesses, threw great light on the subject.

'Friend,' quo' I to him, resting my arms and elbows on the table, and my chin upon the back of my hands,—'did your mock-doctor vend medicines?'

'Oh, yes!' said the man; 'he had pill-boxes and salves.'

'And nothing else?' said I, seeing him hesitate.

'There was a wrapped-up paper.'

'Ay; and what was in it?'

'It was a printed note, saying that the doctor would be consulted by the freemen and their families gratis, every day till the election was over.'

'This looks serious!' exclaimed my Rhadamanthian friend; and I thereupon said to the witness,—'And what was the result?'

'All,' quo' he, 'that consulted the doctor, it was said, were inoculated.'

'What do you mean by inoculated?'

'At the election they all voted for Mr. Gabblon.'

'Well, my friend, but what had Mr. Gabblon to do with that?' and, on saying this, I turned round to the chairman and said, 'The doctor and the merry-andrew should be called before us as witnesses.'

Upon which Mr. Gabblon's lawyer objected, saying, 'They could not be legal witnesses, inasmuch as they were rogues and vagabonds by law.'

This was, however, overruled; and I saw Mr. Gabblon turn of a pallid hue when it was determined to bring them before us.

We then adjourned to afford time, and in due season met again. The doctor and his fool were really very decent, just as respectable to look at as any member of the committee: the merry-andrew was dressed in the tip-top of the fashion, with an eye-glass, hung by a garter-blue riband. But what surprised me most was, that I was some time of discerning in him the same young man that had been so serviceable to Mr. Tough at my own election.

As it was evident to the meanest capacity in the committee, that the inoculation had been performed by matter obtained from Mr. Gabblon, I made a dead set at that point, and said to the clown in a conversible manner:

'And so, my old friend, for I see you are such, we have rather a knotty business in hand: what said the doctor, your master, to you when he mentioned that you were hired to play your pranks for the edification of the good people of Wordam, as you were once hired by a friend of mine to do for me at Frailtown?'

'He said,' replied the young man very becomingly, 'that I should have five guineas.'

'Well, considering your talent, that was moderate; but I don't think you have improved in prudence since we met; for, according to report, you had as much from my friend for one day as for all the seven you performed for Mr. Gabblon.'

'But, sir,' replied the witness, nettled at the idea of his prudence being called in question, 'I had five guineas every day.'

'Oh! I thought you only performed one day.'

'Yes, sir, only one day in public; but the private practice was no easy job.'

'No doubt,' said I; 'but what was this private practice?'

'It was bamboozling the natives before some of them were in a condition to take the doctor's drugs.'

'That was hard work, no doubt; but what was the doctor's medicine that the patients were so loath to take? To be sure drugs are very odious things.'

'I never saw him administer any.'

'You're a clever lad,' said I, 'and you'll just step aside and let the doctor come forward'; which being accordingly done, I continued:

'Doctor,' quo' I, 'I hope you're very well, and have been this long time; you keep your looks very well: no doubt you take a good deal of the same physic that your young man has been telling us was administered, *pro bono publico* and Mr. Gabblon, at Wordam.'

'Not so much as I could wish,' replied the doctor; 'times are very hard.'

'No doubt they are; but what were the doses that operated so efficaciously at Wordam?'

'The Melham bank,' replied the doctor, 'had stopped payment.'

'Hey!'

Mr. Gabblon gave a deep despairing sigh, and I said,

'Doctor, not to trouble you with these trifling questions, for I am sure your medicine was as precious as gold——'

'It was all sovereigns, for the cause I mentioned.'

Mr. Gabblon gave another sigh, and his lawyer, albeit of a rosy hue, turned for a moment white as his wig, and then laughed.

'Doctor,' was my comment, 'we are very much obliged to you; your answers have been exceedingly satisfactory: but one point; it's of no consequence; you should however have mentioned it; and that is, how you got the sovereigns.'

'Oh! Mr. Gabblon's groom brought them every morning, and staid with me as long as patients came.'

'I daresay, doctor, you had many doubtful cases—what was the prevailing complaint?'

At these words, Mr. Gabblon, not the wisest of mankind, suddenly started up, and called the doctor an ass, not to see how I was making a fool of him.

''Tis you,' said the clown, 'that he's making a fool of'; at the same time winking to the Committee with one of his stage faces, forgetful where he was.

In short, not to lengthen my story into tediousness, bribery and corruption was clearly proven; and Mr. Gabblon, as I have already stated, was set aside; for he was not cunning enough, in a parliamentary sense, to be honest,—a thing which leads me to make an observation here, namely, that it is by no means plain why paying for an individual vote should be so much more heinous than paying for a whole borough.

[from *The Member*, in the Canongate Classics omnibus edition, *The Member and The Radical*, pp. 101–4]

ELIZABETH GRANT

Plots and Deceptions

from MEMOIRS OF A HIGHLAND LADY

ELIZABETH GRANT (1797–1885) of Rothiemurchus on Speyside wrote her memoirs for the private enlightenment of her family, and the Canongate Classics volume is the first complete and authentic edition of a racy, honest and entertaining autobiography rich in character, wit, and vivid information. This account of mean tricks played first by a favourite aunt on Elizabeth, and then by the children on an unpopular governess, relates to the year 1808.

We all loved Aunt Mary, not as we had loved Aunt Lissy—she did not merit the same unreserved affection and children know just as well as older people how to appreciate character. Aunt Lissy was thoroughly truthful, uncompromisingly truthful, she had no idea of deception of any kind. Aunt Mary was not so honestly simple. She had company manners and company temper and company conversation like my Mother, all put on with their company dress. We were never certain that either of them meant what they said on these state occasions, even though a smile of softness preceding sweet gentle words were part of the pantomime. To *appear* this that or the other, to *acquit* oneself well, was the Ironside endeavour, so different from the straightforward Grant way of just being what one seemed. Aunt Mary, too, kind and good and amusing as we generally found her, was not strictly just. We were punished sometimes for being in the way more than for having done wrong, her punishments were not always well advised. Amongst several similar transactions the affair of the Workbox, as Jane and I always called it, when sitting in judgement on this circumstance of my life, made a great impression to her disadvantage. Children can define the limits between right and wrong very correctly. My Uncle Frere in his courting

27

days at Twyford had given me a workbox with a lock and key, the first key I had ever possessed—of course to the quick feelings of a sensitive child this was a treasure invaluable. The box had a sliding lid on the outside of which was painted a very full rigged ship sailing over very mountainous waves. It was divided within into many small compartments, certainly particularly suited to Aunt Mary's favourite patch work—all those little nests she said would so exactly hold the different cuttings of her chintzes and papers. Had she asked me to lend the box, although my dolls' rags were already in it and the lid locked safely down and the key on a ribbon round my neck, I should have been pleased to have been useful to her, proud to oblige her, but she set to work otherwise. She waited for my first fault, not long in coming I daresay, and decreed as a punishment the loss of my workbox for so many weeks—an unlimited number it proved, for it never was returned to me from the moment when in an agony of tears and sobs and stifled passion I had to deliver up my key. The patches were immediately installed in all the neat divisions and there they may have remained for years for all that I knew or cared, for my corruption rose and pride or anger prevented my ever alluding to this 'unprincipled affair' again. Still we loved our Aunt and soon had reason to regret her. Mrs Millar, with no eye over her, ruled again, and as winter approached and we were more in the house, nursery troubles were renewed. My father had to be frequently appealed to, severities were resumed. One day William was locked up in a small room used for this pleasant purpose, the next day it was I, bread and water the fare of both. A review of the Volunteers seldom saw us all collected on the ground, there was sure to be one naughty child in prison at home. We were flogged too for every errour, girls and boys alike, but my father permitted no one to strike us but himself. My Mother's occasional slaps and boxes were mere interjections taken no notice of. It was upon this broken rule that I prepared a scene to rid us of the horrid termagant, whom my Mother with a gentle, self-satisfied sigh announced to all her friends as such a treasure. William was my accomplice, and this was our plan.

My father's dressing closet was next to our sitting nursery, and he, with Raper regularity, made use of it most methodically, dressing at certain stated hours, continuing a certain almost fixed time at his toilette, very seldom indeed deviating from this routine, which all in the house were as well aware of as we were, Mrs Millar among the rest. The nursery was very quiet while he was our neighbour. It did sometimes happen, however, that he ran up from his study to the dressing room at unwonted hours, and upon this chance our scheme was founded. William was to watch for this opportunity; as soon as it occurred he secretly warned me, and I immediately became naughty, did something that I knew would be particularly disagreeable to Mrs Millar. She found fault pretty sharply, I replied very pertly, in fact as saucily as I could, and no one could do it better. This was followed as I expected by two or three hard slaps on the back of my neck, upon which I set up a scream worthy of the rest of the scene, so loud, so piercing, that in came my father to find me crouching beneath the claws of a fury. 'I have long suspected this, Millar,' said he, in the cold voice that sunk the heart of every culprit, for the first tone uttered told them that their doom was sealed. 'Six weeks ago I warned you of what would be the consequences; you can retire and pack up your clothes without delay, in an hour you leave this for Aviemore,'—and she did. No entreaties from my Mother, no tears from the three petted younger children, no excuses of any sort availed. In an hour this odious woman had left us for ever. I can't remember her wicked temper now without shuddering at all I went through under her care. In her character, though my father insisted on mentioning the cause for which she was dismissed, my Mother had gifted her with such a catalogue of excellences, that the next time we heard of her she was nurse to the young Duke of Roxburghe—that wonder! long looked for, come at last—and nearly murdered him one day, keeping him under water for some childish fault till he was nearly drowned, quite insensible when taken out by the footman who attended him. After this she was sent to a lunatick asylum, where the poor creature ended her stormy days; her mind had probably always been too unsettled to bear opposition, and we were too old as well as too spirited to have been left so long at the mercy of an ignorant woman, who was really a tender nurse to an infant then. In some respects we were hardly as comfortable without her as with her, the good natured highland girl who replaced her not understanding the neatnesses we had been accustomed to. And then I, like other patriots, had to bear the blame of all these inconveniences; I, who for all our sakes had borne these sharp slaps in order to secure our freedom, was now complained of as the cause of very minor evils. My little brothers and sisters, even William my associate, agreeing that my passionate temper aggravated 'poor Millar,' who had always been 'very kind' to them. Such ingratitude—'Kill the next tiger yourselves,' said I, and withdrew from their questionable society for half a day, by which time Jane having referred the story of the soldier and the brahmin in our *Evenings at home*, and thought the matter over, made an oration which restored outward harmony; inwardly, I remained a little longer angry—another half day—a long period in our estimate of time.

[from *Memoirs of a Highland Lady*, vol 1, pp. 101-4]

JOHN MUIR

Stickeen and the Crevasse

from STICKEEN

JOHN MUIR (1838–1914) was born and raised in Dunbar.
The family moved to Wisconsin in 1849, where Muir
became a naturalist, tireless walker, and campaigner for
National Parks, which were finally established in 1890.

Stickeen deals with an expedition he made through
Alaska in 1880, accompanied by an intrepid mongrel
who emerges as a character of obstinate charm and
originality. The name Stickeen, we are told, was given
to the dog when adopted by the Stickeen Indians, who
regarded him as a mysterious source of wisdom.

Some crevasses remain open for months or even years,
and by the melting of their sides continue to increase in
width long after the opening strain has ceased; while the
sliver-bridges, level on top at first and perfectly safe, are
at length melted to thin, vertical, knife-edged blades, the
upper portion being most exposed to the weather; and since
the exposure is greatest in the middle, they at length curve
downward like the cables of suspension bridges. This one
was evidently very old, for it had been weathered and wasted
until it was the most dangerous and inaccessible that ever lay
in my way. The width of the crevasse was here about fifty
feet, and the sliver crossing diagonally was about seventy
feet long; its thin knife-edge near the middle was depressed
twenty-five or thirty feet below the level of the glacier, and
the upcurving ends were attached to the sides eight or ten
feet below the brink. Getting down the nearly vertical wall
to the end of the sliver and up the other side were the main
difficulties, and they seemed all but insurmountable. Of
the many perils encountered in my years of wandering on
mountains and glaciers none seemed so plain and stern and
merciless as this. And it was presented when we were wet to
the skin and hungry, the sky dark with quick driving snow,

and the night near. But we were forced to face it. It was a tremendous necessity.

Beginning, not immediately above the sunken end of the bridge, but a little to one side, I cut a deep hollow on the brink for my knees to rest in. Then, leaning over, with my shorthandled axe I cut a step sixteen or eighteen inches below, which on account of the sheerness of the wall was necessarily shallow. That step, however, was well made; its floor sloped slightly inward and formed a good hold for my heels. Then, slipping cautiously upon it, and crouching as low as possible, with my left side toward the wall, I steadied myself against the wind with my left hand in a slight notch, while with the right I cut other similar steps and notches in succession, guarding against losing balance by glinting of the axe, or by wind-gusts, for life and death were in every stroke and in the niceness of finish of every foothold.

After the end of the bridge was reached I chipped it down until I had made a level platform six or eight inches wide, and it was a trying thing to poise on this little slipper platform while bending over to get safely astride of the sliver. Crossing was then comparatively easy by chipping off the sharp edge with short, careful strokes, and hitching forward an inch or two at a time, keeping my balance with my knees pressed against the sides. The tremendous abyss on either hand I studiously ignored. To me the edge of that blue sliver was then all the world. But the most trying part of the adventure, after working my way across inch by inch and chipping another small platform, was to rise from the safe position and to cut a step-ladder in the nearly vertical face of the wall,—chipping, climbing, holding on with feet and fingers in mere notches. At such times one's whole body is eye, and common skill and fortitude are replaced by power beyond our call or knowledge. Never before had I been so long under deadly strain. How I got up that cliff I never could tell. The thing seemed to have been done by somebody else. I never have held death in contempt, though in the course of my explorations I have oftentimes felt that to meet one's fate on a noble mountain, or in the heart of a glacier, would be blessed as compared with death from disease, or from some shabby lowland accident. But the best death, quick and crystal-pure, set so glaringly open before us, is hard enough to face, even though we feel gratefully sure that we have already had happiness enough for a dozen lives.

But poor Stickeen, the wee, hairy, sleekit beastie, think of him! When I had decided to dare the bridge, and while I was on my knees chipping a hollow on the rounded brow above it, he came behind me, pushed his head past my shoulder, looked down and across, scanned the sliver and its approaches with his mysterious eyes, then looked me in the face with a startled air of surprise and concern, and began to mutter and whine; saying as plainly as if speaking with words, 'Surely, you are not going into that awful place.' This was the first time I had seen him gaze deliberately into a crevasse, or into my face with an eager, speaking, troubled look. That he should have recognized and appreciated the danger at the first glance showed wonderful sagacity. Never before had the daring midget seemed to know that ice was slippery or that there was any such thing as danger anywhere. His looks and tones of voice when he began to complain and speak his fears were so human that I unconsciously talked to him in sympathy as I would to a frightened boy, and in trying to calm his fears perhaps in some measure moderated my own. 'Hush your fears, my boy,' I said, 'we will get across it safe, though it is not going to be easy. No right way is easy in this rough world. We must risk our lives to save them. At the worst we can only slip, and then how grand a grave we will have, and by and by our nice bones will do good in the terminal moraine.'

But my sermon was far from reassuring him: he began to cry, and after taking another piercing look at the tremendous gulf, ran away in desperate excitement, seeking some other crossing. By the time he got back, baffled of course, I had made a step or two. I dared not look back, but he made himself heard; and when he saw that I was certainly bent on crossing he cried aloud in despair. The danger was enough to daunt anybody, but it seems wonderful that he should have been able to weigh and appreciate it so justly. No mountaineer could have seen it more quickly or judged it more wisely, discriminating between real and apparent peril.

When I gained the other side, he screamed louder than ever, and after running back and forth in vain search for a way of escape, he would return to the brink of the crevasse above the bridge, moaning and wailing as if in the bitterness of death. Could this be the silent, philosophic Stickeen? I shouted encouragement, telling him the bridge was not so bad as it looked, that I had left it flat and safe for his feet, and he could walk it easily. But he was afraid to try. Strange so small an animal should be capable of such big, wise fears. I called again and again in a reassuring tone to come on and fear nothing; that he could come if he would only try. He would hush for a moment, look down again at the bridge, and shout his unshakable conviction that he could never, never come that way; then lie back in despair, as if howling, 'O-o-oh! What a place! No-o-o, I can never go-o-o down there!' His natural composure and courage had vanished utterly in a tumultuous storm of fear. Had the danger been less, his distress would have seemed ridiculous. But in this dismal, merciless abyss lay the shadow of death, and his heartrending cries might well have called Heaven to his help. Perhaps they did. So hidden before, he was now transparent, and one could see the workings of his heart and mind like the movements of a clock out of its case. His voice and gestures, hopes and fears, were so perfectly human that none could mistake them; while he seemed to understand every word of mine. I was troubled at the thought of having to leave him out all night, and of the danger of not finding him in the morning. It seemed impossible to get him to venture. To compel him to try through fear of being abandoned, I started off as if leaving him to his fate, and disappeared back of a hummock; but this did no good; he only lay down and moaned in utter hopeless misery. So, after hiding a few minutes, I went back to the brink of the crevasse and in a severe tone of voice shouted across to him that now I must certainly leave him, I could wait no longer, and that, if he would not come, all I could promise was that I would return to seek him next day. I warned him that if he went back to the woods the wolves would kill him, and finished by urging him once more by words and gestures to come on, come on.

He knew very well what I meant, and at last, with the courage of despair, hushed and breathless, he crouched down on the brink in the hollow I had made for my knees, pressed his body against the ice as if trying to get the advantage of the friction of every hair, gazed into the first step, put his little feet together and slid them slowly, slowly over the edge and down into it, bunching all four in it and almost standing on his head. Then, without lifting his feet, as well as I could see through the snow, he slowly worked them over the edge of the step and down into the next and the next in succession in the same way, and gained the end of the bridge. Then, lifting his feet with the regularity and slowness of the vibrations of a seconds pendulum, as if counting and measuring *one-two-three*, holding himself steady against the gusty wind, and giving separate attention to each little step, he gained the foot of the cliff, while I was on my knees leaning over to give him a lift should he succeed in getting within reach of my arm. Here he halted in dead silence, and it was here I feared he might fail, for dogs are poor climbers. I had no cord. If I had had one, I would have dropped a noose over his head and hauled him up. But while I was thinking whether an available cord might be made out of clothing, he was looking keenly into the series of notched steps and finger-holds I had made, as if counting them, and fixing the position of each one of them in his mind. Then suddenly up he came in a springy rush, hooking his paws into the steps and notches so quickly that I could not see how it was done, and whizzed past my head, safe at last!

And now came a scene! 'Well done, well done, little boy! Brave boy!' I cried, trying to catch and caress him; but he would not be caught. Never before or since have I seen anything like so passionate a revulsion from the depths of despair to exultant, triumphant, uncontrollable joy. He flashed and darted hither and thither as if fairly demented, screaming and shouting, swirling round and round in giddy loops and circles like a leaf in a whirlwind, lying down, and rolling over and over, sidewise and heels over head, and pouring forth a tumultuous flood of hysterical cries and sobs and gasping mutterings. When I ran up to him to shake him, fearing he might die of joy, he flashed off two or three hundred yards, his feet in a mist of motion; then, turning suddenly, came back in a wild rush and launched himself at my face, almost knocking me down, all the time screeching and screaming and shouting as if saying, 'Saved! saved! saved!' Then away again, dropping suddenly at times with his feet in the air, trembling and fairly sobbing. Such passionate emotion was enough to kill him. Moses' stately song of triumph after escaping the Egyptians and the Red Sea was nothing to it. Who could have guessed the capacity of the dull, enduring little fellow for all that most stirs this mortal frame? Nobody could have helped crying with him!

[from *Stickeen*, pp. 13–18 in the Canongate Classics omnibus edition, *The Wilderness Journeys*]

Taking a Wife
from 'The Beach of Falesá'

ROBERT LOUIS STEVENSON (1850–94) was born and educated in Edinburgh, the son and grandson of lighthouse-builders. His Scottish novels have long been accepted as classics, while his novella *Dr Jekyll and Mr Hyde* is one of those books which have influenced thousands who never read it. Yet his South Seas tales have never received equal attention.

'The Beach of Falesá', from which this extract is taken, shows a remarkable grasp of rough dialogue, action and psychology, as well as the most supple story-telling skill.

A trader new to the islands falls in with a parcel of local scoundrels led by a man named Case . . .

'By the by,' says Case, 'we must get you a wife.'

'That's so,' said I, 'I had forgotten.'

There was a crowd of girls about us, and I pulled myself up and looked among them like a Bashaw. They were all dressed out for the sake of the ship being in; and the women of Falesá are a handsome lot to see. If they have a fault, they are a trifle broad in the beam; and I was just thinking so when Case touched me.

'That's pretty,' says he.

I saw one coming on the other side alone. She had been fishing; all she wore was a chemise, and it was wetted through, and a cutty sark at that. She was young and very slender for an island maid, with a long face, a high forehead, and a sly, strange, blindish look between a cat's and a baby's.

'Who's she?' said I. 'She'll do.'

'That's Uma,' said Case, and he called her up and spoke to her in the native. I didn't know what he said; but when he was in the midst, she looked up at me quick and timid like a child dodging a blow; then down again; and presently smiled. She had a wide mouth, the lips and the chin cut like any statue's; and the smile came out for a moment and was gone. There she stood with her head bent and heard Case to an end; spoke back in the pretty Polynesian voice, looking him full in the face; heard him again in answer; and then with an obeisance started off. I had just a share of the bow, but never another shot of her eye; and there was no more word of smiling.

'I guess it's all right,' said Case. 'I guess you can have her. I'll make it square with the old lady. You can have your pick of the lot for a plug of tobacco,' he added, sneering.

I suppose it was the smile stuck in my memory, for I spoke back sharp. 'She doesn't look that sort,' I cried.

'I don't know that she is,' said Case. 'I believe she's as right as the mail. Keeps to herself, don't go round with the gang, and that. O, no, don't you misunderstand me—Uma's on the square.' He spoke eager I thought, and that surprised and pleased me. 'Indeed,' he went on, 'I shouldn't make so sure of getting her, only she cottoned to the cut of your jib. All you have to do is to keep dark and let me work the mother my own way; and I'll bring the girl round to the captain's for the marriage.'

I didn't care for the word marriage, and I said so.

'O, there's nothing to hurt in the marriage,' says he. 'Black Jack's the chaplain.'

By this time we had come in view of the house of these three white men; for a negro is counted a white man—and so is a Chinese! a strange idea, but common in the islands. It was a board house with a strip of ricketty verandah. The store was to the front, with a counter, scales and the poorest possible display of trades: a case or two of tinned meats; a barrel of hard bread; a few bolts of cotton stuff, not to be compared with mine; the only thing well represented being the contraband—fire arms and liquor. 'If these are my only rivals,' thinks I, 'I should do well in Falesá.' Indeed there was only the one way they could touch me, and that was with the guns and drink.

In the back room was old Captain Randall, squatting on the floor native fashion, fat and pale, naked to the waist, gray as a badger and his eyes set with drink. His body was covered with gray hair and crawled over by flies; one was in the corner of his eye—he never heeded; and the mosquitoes hummed about the man like bees. Any clean-minded man would have had the creature out at once and buried him; and to see him, and think he was seventy, and remember he had once commanded a ship, and come ashore in his smart togs, and talked big in bars and consulates, and sat in club verandahs, turned me sick and sober.

He tried to get up when I came in, but that was hopeless, so he reached me a hand instead and stumbled out some salutation.

'Papa's pretty full this morning,' observed Case. 'We've had an epidemic here; and Captain Randall takes gin for a prophylactic—don't you, papa?'

'Never took such thing my life!' cried the captain, indignantly. 'Take gin for my health's sake, Mr Wha's-ever-your-name. 'S a preacaution'ry measure.'

'That's all right, papa,' said Case. 'But you'll have to brace up. There's going to be a marriage, Mr Wiltshire here is going to get spliced.'

The old man asked to whom.

'To Uma,' said Case.

'Uma?' cried the captain. 'Wha's he want Uma for? 'S he come here for his health, anyway? Wha' 'n hell's he want Uma for?'

'Dry up papa,' said Case. 'Tain't you that's to marry her. I guess you're not her godfather and godmother, I guess Mr Wiltshire's going to please himself.'

With that he made an excuse to me that he must move about the marriage, and left me alone with the poor wretch that was his partner and (to speak truth) his gull. Trade and station belonged both to Randall; Case and the negro were parasites; they crawled and fed upon him like the flies, he none the wiser. Indeed I have no harm to say of Billy Randall, beyond the fact that my gorge rose at him, and the time I now passed in his company was like a nightmare.

The room was stifling hot and full of flies; for the house was dirty and low and small, and stood in a bad place, behind the village, in the borders of the bush, and sheltered from the

trade. The three men's beds were on the floor, and a litter of
pans and dishes. There was no standing furniture, Randall,
when he was violent, tearing it to laths. There I sat, and
had a meal which was served us by Case's wife; and there
I was entertained all day by that remains of man, his tongue
stumbling among low old jokes and long old stories, and his
own wheezy laughter always ready, so that he had no sense
of depression. He was nipping gin all the while; sometimes
he fell asleep and awoke again whimpering and shivering,
and every now and again he would ask me why in Hell I
wanted to marry Uma. 'My friend,' I was telling myself all
day, 'you must not be an old gentleman like this.'

It might be four in the afternoon perhaps, when the
backdoor was thrust slowly open, and a strange old native
woman crawled into the house almost on her belly. She
was swathed in black stuff to her heels; her hair was gray in
swatches; her face was tattooed, which was not the practise
in that island; her eyes big and bright and crazy. These
she fixed upon me with a wrapt expression that I saw to
be part acting; she said no plain word, but smacked and
mumbled with her lips, and hummed aloud, like a child
over its Christmas pudding. She came straight across the
house heading for me, and as soon as she was alongside,
caught up my hand and purred and crooned over it like a
great cat. From this she slipped into a kind of song.

'Who in the devil's this?' cried I, for the thing startled
me.

'It's Faavao,' says Randall, and I saw he had hitched
along the floor into the farthest corner.

'You ain't afraid of her?' I cried.

'Me 'fraid!' cried the captain. 'My dear friend, I defy her!
I don't let her put her foot in here. Only I suppose 's diff'ent
today for the marriage. 'S Uma's mother.'

'Well, suppose it is, what's she carrying on about?' I asked,
more irritated, perhaps more frightened than I cared to show;
and the captain told me she was making up a quantity of
poetry in my praise because I was to marry Uma. 'All right,
old lady,' says I, with rather a failure of a laugh. 'Anything
to oblige. But when you're done with my hand, you might
let me know.'

She did as though she understood; the song rose into a cry and stopped; the woman crouched out of the house the same way that she came in, and must have plunged straight into the bush, for when I followed her to the door she had already vanished.

'These are rum manners,' said I.

''S a rum crowd,' said the captain, and to my surprise he made the sign of the cross on his bare bosom.

[from 'The Beach of Falesá' in *Island Landfalls*, pp. 167–70 in the Canongate Classics omnibus edition, *Tales of the South Seas*]

ARTHUR CONAN DOYLE

The Medal

from THE EXPLOITS OF BRIGADIER GERARD

ARTHUR CONAN DOYLE (1859–1930) was born in
Edinburgh, and trained there as a doctor, practising
in the south of England until 1890, when he came into
his own as a writer, publishing in his lifetime over sixty
books, receiving a knighthood in 1902.

Doyle's reputation has been swallowed by that of his
domineering offspring, Sherlock Holmes, yet the deft
tales of Napoleon's flamboyant Brigadier Gerard are
rich in excitement, humour and irony. In this story,
Gerard has been sent with a message through hostile
country, and, as usual, gallantly misses the point.

I have said that at the further end of the cellar there was a dim
grey fan of light striking downwards from somewhere near
the roof. Well, as I peered through the darkness, I suddenly
saw a great, tall man skip into this belt of daylight, and then
out again into the darkness at the further end. My word, I
gave such a start that my busby nearly broke its chin-strap!
It was only a glance, but, none the less, I had time to see that
the fellow had a hairy Cossack cap on his head, and that he
was a great, long-legged, broad-shouldered brigand, with
a sabre at his waist. My faith, even Etienne Gerard was a
little staggered at being left alone with such a creature in
the dark.

But only for a moment. 'Courage!' I thought. 'Am I not
a hussar, a brigadier, too, at the age of thirty-one, and the
chosen messenger of the Emperor?' After all, this skulker
had more cause to be afraid of me than I of him. And then
suddenly I understood that he was afraid—horribly afraid.
I could read it from his quick step and his bent shoulders
as he ran among the barrels, like a rat making for its hole.
And, of course, it must have been he who had held the
door against me, and not some packing-case or wine-cask

as I had imagined. He was the pursued then, and I the pursuer. Aha, I felt my whiskers bristle as I advanced upon him through the darkness! He would find that he had no chicken to deal with, this robber from the North. For the moment I was magnificent.

At first I had feared to light my candle lest I should make a mark of myself, but now, after cracking my shin over a box, and catching my spurs in some canvas, I thought the bolder course the wiser. I lit it therefore, and then I advanced with long strides, my sword in my hand. 'Come out, you rascal!' I cried. 'Nothing can save you. You will at last meet with your deserts.'

I held my candle high, and presently I caught a glimpse of the man's head staring at me over a barrel. He had a gold chevron on his black cap, and the expression of his face told me in an instant that he was an officer and a man of refinement.

'Monsieur,' he cried in excellent French, 'I surrender myself on a promise of quarter. But if I do not have your promise, I will then sell my life as dearly as I can.'

'Sir,' said I, 'a Frenchman knows how to treat an unfortunate enemy. Your life is safe.' With that he handed his sword over the top of the barrel, and I bowed with the candle on my heart. 'Whom have I the honour of capturing?' I asked.

'I am the Count Boutkine, of the Emperor's own Don Cossacks,' said he. 'I came out with my troop to reconnoitre Senlis, and as we found no sign of your people we determined to spend the night here.'

'And would it be an indiscretion,' I asked, 'if I were to inquire how you came into the back cellar?'

'Nothing more simple,' said he. 'It was our intention to start at early dawn. Feeling chilled after dressing, I thought that a cup of wine would do me no harm, so I came down to see what I could find. As I was rummaging about, the house was suddenly carried by assault so rapidly that by the time I had climbed the stairs it was all over. It only remained for me to save myself, so I came down here and hid myself in the back cellar, where you have found me.'

I thought of how old Bouvet had behaved under the same conditions, and the tears sprang to my eyes as I contemplated the glory of France. Then I had to consider what I should do next. It was clear that this Russian Count, being in the back cellar while we were in the front one, had not heard the sounds which would have told him that the house was once again in the hands of his own allies. If he should once understand this the tables would be turned, and I should be his prisoner instead of he being mine. What was I to do? I was at my wits' end, when suddenly there came to me an idea so brilliant that I could not but be amazed at my own invention.

'Count Boutkine,' said I, 'I find myself in a most difficult position.'

'And why?' he asked.

'Because I have promised you your life.' His jaw dropped a little.

'You would not withdraw your promise?' he cried.

'If the worst comes to the worst I can die in your defence,' said I; 'but the difficulties are great.'

'What is it, then?' he asked.

'I will be frank with you,' said I. 'You must know that our fellows, and especially the Poles, are so incensed against the Cossacks that the mere sight of the uniform drives them mad. They precipitate themselves instantly upon the wearer and tear him limb from limb. Even their officers cannot restrain them.'

The Russian grew pale at my words and the way in which I said them.

'But this is terrible,' said he.

'Horrible!' said I. 'If we were to go up together at this moment I cannot promise how far I could protect you.'

'I am in your hands,' he cried. 'What would you suggest that we should do? Would it not be best that I should remain here?'

'That worst of all.'

'And why?'

'Because our fellows will ransack the house presently, and then you would be cut to pieces. No, no, I must go up and break it to them. But even then, when once they see that accursed uniform, I do not know what may happen.'

'Should I then take the uniform off?'

'Excellent!' I cried. 'Hold, we have it! You will take your uniform off and put on mine. That will make you sacred to every French soldier.'

'It is not the French I fear so much as the Poles.'

'But my uniform will be a safeguard against either.'

'How can I thank you?' he cried. 'But you—what are you to wear?'

'I will wear yours.'

'And perhaps fall a victim to your generosity?'

'It is my duty to take the risk,' I answered, 'but I have no fears. I will ascend in your uniform. A hundred swords will be turned upon me. "Hold!" I will shout, "I am the Brigadier Gerard!" Then they will see my face. They will know me. And I will tell them about you. Under the shield of these clothes you will be sacred.'

His fingers trembled with eagerness as he tore off his tunic. His boots and breeches were much like my own, so there was no need to change them, but I gave him my hussar jacket, my dolman, my busby, my sword-belt, and my sabre-tasche, while I took in exchange his high sheepskin cap with the gold chevron, his fur-trimmed coat, and his crooked sword. Be it well understood that in changing the tunics I did not forget to change my thrice-precious letter also from my old one to my new.

'With your leave,' said I, 'I shall now bind you to a barrel.'

. . .

When I had got as far as Dammartin I caught a first glimpse of our own outposts. There was a troop of dragoons in a field, and of course I could see from the horsehair crests that they were French. I galloped towards them in order to ask them if all was safe between there and Paris, and as I rode I felt such a pride at having won my way back to my friends again, that I could not refrain from waving my sword in the air.

At this a young officer galloped out from among the dragoons, also brandishing his sword, and it warmed my heart to think that he should come riding with such ardour and enthusiasm to greet me. I made Violette caracole, and as we came together I brandished my sword more gallantly than ever, but you can imagine my feelings when he suddenly made a cut at me which would certainly have taken my head off if I had not fallen forward with my nose in Violette's mane. My faith, it whistled just over my cap like an east wind. Of course, it came from this accursed Cossack uniform which, in my excitement, I had forgotten all about, and this young dragoon had imagined that I was some Russian champion who was challenging the French cavalry. My word, he was a frightened man when he understood how near he had been to killing the celebrated Brigadier Gerard.

. . .

When I came to the headquarters I was shown straight into the Emperor's room. He was drinking coffee at a writing-table, with a big plan drawn out on paper in front of him. Berthier and Macdonald were leaning, one over each shoulder, and he was talking so quickly that I don't believe that either of them could catch a half of what he was saying. But when his eyes fell upon me he dropped the pen on to the chart, and he sprang up with a look in his pale face which struck me cold.

'What the deuce are you doing here?' he shouted. When he was angry he had a voice like a peacock.

'I have the honour to report to you, sire,' said I, 'that I have delivered your despatch safely to the King of Spain.'

'What!' he yelled, and his two eyes transfixed me like bayonets. Oh, those dreadful eyes, shifting from grey to blue, like steel in the sunshine. I can see them now when I have a bad dream.

'What has become of Charpentier?' he asked.

'He is captured,' said Macdonald.

'By whom?'

'The Russians.'

'The Cossacks?'

'No, a single Cossack.'

'He gave himself up?'

'Without resistance.'

'He is an intelligent officer. You will see that the medal of honour is awarded to him.'

When I heard those words I had to rub my eyes to make sure that I was awake.

'As to you,' cried the Emperor, taking a step forward as if he would have struck me, 'you brain of a hare, what do you think that you were sent upon this mission for? Do you conceive that I would send a really important message by such a hand as yours, and through every village which the enemy holds? How you came through them passes my comprehension; but if your fellow messenger had had but as little sense as you, my whole plan of campaign would have been ruined. Can you not see, coglione, that this message contained false news, and that it was intended to deceive the enemy whilst I put a very different scheme into execution?'

When I heard those cruel words and saw the angry, white face which glared at me, I had to hold the back of a chair, for my mind was failing me and my knees would hardly bear me up. But then I took courage as I reflected that I was an honourable gentleman, and that my whole life had been spent in toiling for this man and for my beloved country.

'Sire,' said I, and the tears would trickle down my cheeks whilst I spoke, 'when you are dealing with a man like me you would find it wiser to deal openly. Had I known that you had wished the despatch to fall into the hands of the enemy, I would have seen that it came there. As I believed that I was to guard it, I was prepared to sacrifice my life for it. I do not believe, sire, that any man in the world ever met with more toils and perils than I have done in trying to carry out what I thought was your will.'

I dashed the tears from my eyes as I spoke, and with such fire and spirit as I could command I gave him an account of it all, of my dash through Soissons, my brush with the dragoons, my adventure in Senlis, my reconnoitre with Count Boutkine in the cellar, my disguise, my meeting with the Cossack officer, my flight, and how at the last moment I was nearly cut down by a French dragoon. The Emperor, Berthier, and Macdonald listened with astonishment on their faces. When I had finished Napoleon stepped forward and he pinched me by the ear.

'There, there!' said he. 'Forget anything which I may have said. I would have done better to trust you. You may go.'

I turned to the door, and my hand was upon the handle, when the Emperor called upon me to stop.

'You will see,' said he, turning to the Duke of Tarentum, 'that Brigadier Gerard has the special medal of honour, for I believe that if he has the thickest head he has also the stoutest heart in my army.'

[from *The Exploits of Brigadier Gerard* in the Canongate Classics omnibus edition, *The Complete Brigadier Gerard*, pp. 28–39]

Wounded Feelings

from THE HOUSE WITH THE GREEN SHUTTERS

GEORGE DOUGLAS BROWN was born in Ayrshire in 1869, and died after a brief life of promise and frustration, aged thirty-three, leaving only *The House with the Green Shutters* as a serious contribution to Scottish literature. A mordant account of small-town life, often close to satire, it is written with a sharp bite and brilliance which makes us painfully aware of Brown's potential. The book itself can be taken as an attack on a narrowness in Scottish life which perverts and inhibits creative talent, yet proved, ironically, to be prelude and inspiration for the wild flowering of just such talent later in the twentieth century.

Gourlay is the ambitious bully who seeks to dominate the life of Barbie, and whose overweening ambition leads to disaster. When this extract begins he has just dismissed his servant, Jock Gilmour.

'I'll wager ye,' cried Johnny Coe quickly, speaking more loudly than usual in the animation of discovery. 'I'll wager ye Gourlay has quarrelled him and put him to the door!'

'Man, you're right! that'll just be it, that'll just be it! Aye; aye; faith aye; and yon'll be his kist he's carrying! Man, you're right, Mr Coe; you have just put your finger on't. We'll hear news *this* morning.'

They edged forward to the middle of the road, the Provost in front, to meet Gilmour coming down.

'Ye've a heavy burden this morning, John,' said the Provost graciously.

'No wonder, sir,' said Gilmour with big-eyed solemnity, and set down the chest; 'it's no wonder, seeing that I'm carrying my a-all.'

'Aye, man, John. How's that na?'

To be the centre of interest and the object of gracious condescension was balm to the wounded feelings of

Gilmour. Gourlay had lowered him, but this reception restored him to his own good opinion. He was usually called 'Jock' (except by his mother, to whom, of course, he was 'oor Johnny') but the best merchants in the town were addressing him as 'John'. It was a great occasion. Gilmour expanded in gossip beneath its influence benign.

He welcomed, too, this first and fine opportunity of venting his wrath on the Gourlays.

'Oh, I just telled Gourlay what I thocht of him, and took the door ahint me. I let him have it hot and hardy, I can tell ye. He'll no' forget *me* in a hurry'—Gilmour bawled angrily, and nodded his head significantly, and glared fiercely, to show what good cause he had given Gourlay to remember him—'he'll no forget *me* for a month of Sundays.'

'Aye, man, John, what did ye say till him?'

'Na, man, what did he say to you?'

'Wath he angry, Dyohn?'

'How did the thing begin?'

'Tell us, man, John.'

'What was it a-all about, John?'

'Was Mrs Gourlay there?'

Bewildered by this pelt of questions Gilmour answered the last that hit his ear. 'There, aye; faith, she was there. It was her was the cause o't.'

'D'ye tell me that, John? Man, you surprise me. I would have thocht the thowless trauchle[1] hadna the smeddum left to interfere.'

'Oh, it was yon boy of hers. He's aye swaggerin' aboot, interferin' wi' folk at their wark—he follows his faither's example in that, for as the auld cock crows the young ane learns—and his mither's that daft aboot him that ye daurna give a look! He came in my road when I was sweeping out the close, and some o' the dirty jaups splashed about his shins; but was I to blame for that?—ye maun walk wide o' a whalebone besom if ye dinna want to be splashed. Afore I kenned where I was, he up wi' a dirty washing-clout and slashed me in the face wi't! I hit him a thud in the ear—as wha wadna? Out come his mither like a fury, skirling about

[1] Trauchle, *a poor trollop who trails about;* smeddum, *grit.*

her hoose, and *her* servants, and *her* weans. "Your servant!"
says I, "your servant! You're a nice-looking trollop to talk
aboot servants," says I.'

'Did ye really, John?'

'Man, that wath bauld o' ye.'

'And what did *she* say?'

'Oh, she just kept skirling! And then, to be sure, Gourlay
must come out and interfere! But I telled him to his face
what I thocht of *him*! "The best Gourlay that ever dirtied
leather," says I, "'s no gaun to make dirt of me," says I.'

'Aye man, Dyohn!' lisped Deacon Allardyce, with bright
and eagerly inquiring eyes. 'And what did he thay to that, na?
That wath a dig for him! I'the warrant he wath angry.'

'Angry? He foamed at the mouth! But I up and says to
him, "I have had enough o' you," says I, "you and your
Hoose wi' the Green Shutters," says I, "you're no fit to
have a decent servant," says I. "Pay *me my* wages and I'll
be redd o' ye," says I. And wi' that I flang my kist on my
shouther and slapped the gate ahint me.'

'And *did* he pay ye your wages?' Tam Wylie probed him
slyly, with a sideward glimmer in his eye.

'Ah, well, no; not exactly,' said Gilmour drawing in. 'But
I'll get them right enough for a' that. He'll no get the better
o' *me*.' Having grounded unpleasantly on the question of the
wages he thought it best to be off ere the bloom was dashed
from his importance, so he shouldered his chest and went.
The bodies watched him down the street.

'He's a lying brose, that,' said the baker.

[from *The House with the Green Shutters*, pp. 30–2]

The Far Islands

from THE WATCHER BY THE THRESHOLD:
SHORTER SCOTTISH FICTION

JOHN BUCHAN (1875–1940) was a son of the Free Church
Manse who became Governor-General of Canada and,
of lesser importance in his eyes, the author of classic
adventure stories. Brought up to Calvinism, he adopted
at Oxford the study of rationalist philosophy, and then
the social assumptions of the English Establishment,
but remained at heart a writer, and one with a strong
sense of something hidden and unattained.

His early story, 'The Far Islands', from which this
extract is taken, concerns a man troubled from childhood
by visions of an island beyond the sea, which he is
always trying to reach. The vision is lost, but returns at
unexpected moments, like the door in the wall in H.G.
Wells' story of that name. Some of Buchan's shorter
tales balance the extrovert adventure thrillers and bring
to mind his final book, *Sick Heart River*.

A childish illness brought Colin to Kinlochuna when he
had reached the mature age of five, and delicate health kept
him there for the greater part of the next six years. During
the winter he lived in London, but from the late northern
spring, through all the long bright summers, he lived in
the great tenantless place without company—for he was an
only child. A French nurse had the charge of his doings, and
when he had passed through the formality of lessons there
were the long pinewoods at his disposal, the rough moor,
the wonderful black holes with the rich black mud in them,
and best of all the bay of Acharra, below the headland, with
Cuna lying in the waves a mile to the west. At such times his
father was busy elsewhere; his mother was dead; the family
had few near relatives; so he passed a solitary childhood in
the company of seagulls and the birds of the moor.

His time for the beach was the afternoon. On the left as you go down through the woods from the house there runs out the great headland of Acharra, red and grey with mosses, and with a nimbus always of screaming sea-fowl. To the right runs a low beach of sand, passing into rough limestone boulders and then into the heather of the wood. This in turn is bounded by a reef of low rocks falling by gentle breaks to the water's edge. It is crowned with a tangle of heath and fern, bright at most seasons with flowers, and dwarf pine-trees straggle on its crest till one sees the meaning of its Gaelic name, 'The Ragged Cock's-Comb'. This place was Colin's playground in fine weather. When it blew rain or snow from the north he dwelt indoors among dogs and books, puzzling his way through great volumes from his father's shelves. But when the mild west-wind weather fell on the sea, then he would lie on the hot sand—Amélie the nurse reading a novel on the nearest rock—and kick his small heels as he followed his fancy. He built great sand castles to the shape of Acharra old tower, and peopled them with preposterous knights and ladies; he drew great moats and rivers for the tide to fill; he fought battles innumerable with crackling seaweed, till Amélie, with her sharp cry of 'Colin, Colin', would carry him houseward for tea.

Two fancies remained in his mind through those boyish years. One was about the mysterious shining sea before him. In certain weathers it seemed to him a solid pathway, Cuna, the little ragged isle, ceased to block the horizon, and his own white road ran away down into the west, till suddenly it stopped and he saw no farther. He knew he ought to see more, but always at one place, just when his thoughts were pacing the white road most gallantly, there came a baffling mist to his sight, and he found himself looking at a commonplace sea with Cuna lying very real and palpable in the offing. It was a vexatious limitation, for all his dreams were about this pathway. One day in June, when the waters slept in a deep heat, he came down the sands barefoot, and lo! there was his pathway. For one moment things seemed clear, the mist had not gathered on the road, and with a cry he ran down to the tide's edge and waded in. The touch of water dispelled the illusion, and almost in tears he saw the crude back of Cuna blotting out his own magic way.

The other fancy was about the low ridge of rocks which bounded the bay on the right. His walks had never extended beyond it, either on the sands or inland, for that way lay a steep hillside and a perilous bog. But often on the sands he had come to its foot and wondered what country lay beyond. He made many efforts to explore it, difficult efforts, for the vigilant Amélie had first to be avoided. Once he was almost at the top when some sea-weed to which he clung gave way, and he rolled back again to the soft warm sand. By-and-by he found that he knew what was beyond. A clear picture had built itself up in his brain of a mile of reefs, with sand in bars between them, and beyond all a sea-wood of alders slipping from the hill's skirts to the water's edge. This was not what he wanted in his explorations, so he stopped, till one day it struck him that the westward view might reveal something beyond the hog-backed Cuna. One day, pioneering alone, he scaled the steepest heights of the sea-weed and pulled his chin over the crest of the ridge. There, sure enough, was his picture—a mile of reefs and the tattered sea-wood. He turned eagerly seawards. Cuna still lay humped on the waters, but beyond it he seemed to see his shining pathway running far to a speck which might be an island. Crazy with pleasure he stared at the vision, till slowly it melted into the waves, and Cuna the inexorable once more blocked the skyline. He climbed down, his heart in a doubt between despondency and hope.

[from 'The Far Islands' in *The Watcher by the Threshold: Shorter Scottish Fiction*, pp. 238–41]

J. MACDOUGALL HAY

Topsail Janet and the Sea
from GILLESPIE

Gillespie was one of the two novels written by the brilliant
and tormented J. MACDOUGALL HAY (1881–1919). It is
a weird, dark, powerful story strongly influenced by
Brown's *House with the Green Shutters*, but wildly different
in style and background, and more deeply metaphysical
in tone.

Brought up in Tarbert on Loch Fyne, Hay was first
a teacher and then a troubled minister of the Church.
He died of tuberculosis aged thirty-eight.

The book deals with the machinations of the power-
hungry Gillespie, and ends like *Green Shutters* in tragedy.
Topsail Janet moves in and out of the story in her own
individual way, one of a rich cast of characters bringing
darkness or light.

When the plumber died Topsail Janet left the house in the
Back Street and took a single room at the Old Quay, whose
window looked into the rusty walls of the beetling Quarry.
In the first year of her bereavement she hovered with a quick
hunger about his grave; but every succeeding Sunday the
grave grew deeper. She prayed that she, too, might die.
She had to take to whelk-gathering, and rarely saw the sun
within her room, for she went out at dawn and returned,
wet and weary to the bone, at lamp-light. Carrying her bag
of whelks she would creep cautiously from the village boys.
'Topsail Janet! Topsail Janet!' they would shout mockingly,
and careering against her would send her staggering forward.
She wore her mother's tippet; and once, when it fluttered
in the breeze, someone said 'Topsail', and the name stuck
to her. For a long time the name burned as a stigma; but
habit made the brand cold.

There was a profound contrast between the parsimony of
her life and the vastness of the sea, her daily companion. She

55

waded at evening in gold-red pools, creeping over the russet tangle, scarce visible save for a fluttering drugget petticoat. At dawn she was a grey toiler on a grey isle, which the tide had given up for a little while, only to drive her shoreward with a gleam of flashing teeth. At times the shore-ice had to be broken; at times the squalls rushed up in black to her feet, and the rain rose along the sea swamping her in misery. To happy people she probably looked picturesque, wading in the salt-water pools or crawling about the rocks, as she plucked here and there a whelk and cast it into a rusty tin can.

She had her own bigness of heart. One day, as she stretched her tired back and gazed vacantly at the bare sea running in white flashes to the empty horizon, the north wind brought her a gift. High in the blue she saw a great rocking bird. It plunged downwards, sheered towards the cliffs, cannoned with a splash of feathers against the wall of stone, and fell among the sea-bent.

Often she had scurried for home, when, in the dusk, the whales arose out of the sea and fluked across the bay. Now she was more greatly scared as she watched the helpless flutter of wings. She divined the beating of the pinions to be death. With her heart choking within her she flew along the lonely shore, hearing the noise of the great wings, as if the shadow of death rustled at her heels. Once, round a sheltering point, she stopped, panting. In the silence she heard the labour of the wings slacken and cease. Her courage returned. The solan would be dead. The sea babbled plaintively on the shore. Everything in the stillness was as it had been. Suddenly there was a sharp scream, child-like with its load of pain. Her heart stood still. Again all was profoundly silent. She peered round the rock, and clutching at her bosom, stumbled forward, and saw a white inert mass. As she crept towards it the solan goose opened its bright eyes and beat the ground with one wing. This sign of life nerved her. She dropped on her knees and saw the white down dappled with blood. The hills began to spin slowly about her and the sea grew dark, when the wing beat again with a feeble spasmodic movement, and a low croak gurgled in the throat of the bird. She thought the sound came through running blood. A fierce wave of

pity swept over her, and she put out her hand and touched
the ruffled neck. At the touch the bird struggled on its side
along the ground. She followed cautiously, wishing that
her hands were less rough. The bird with the beautiful
pinions became holy in her eyes. Taking off her shawl
she wrapped the broken-winged solan in it, tenderly as a
mother her first-born, and held the struggling bundle till it
lay exhausted, her heart crying out at the terror of the bird.
Leaving her bag, her whelks, her all, to the greedy tide she
set off for home, wild with apprehension lest the bird die
in her hands.

Dr. Maclean was called in. He had hurried at the summons
of Topsail, wondering if she had caught pneumonia at last.
When he was told that his patient was a bird he swore in
relief, and bound up the mangled wing.

'Some day, Topsail, you'll fly too,' he said, going out.

She looked at him open-mouthed.

'The Bible says that angels have wings. One of these days
you'll fly out of the window and over the quarry there.'

'Ach! away wi' ye, doctor.'

'That's how you'll go to heaven.'

Part of her small store went to the milk-cart. The sick bird
refused the milk, even though she sweetened it with sugar.
In deep anxiety she watched by it through the long evening,
mending her fire with the best of her drift-wood, and making
a nest for it with a blanket off the bed. In the morning she
consulted Ned o' the Horn, who contemptuously kicked her
saucer aside and ordered fresh herring. She went to the Quay
to beg. The sharp eyes of the bird swung round, needle-like in
their brightness at the smell of the fish, the long sinewy neck
flashed out; in a vast wonder she saw the tail of the herring
vanish. Croak! croak! came the low, glad note of thanks,
going straight to her heart. Herring after herring vanished
in the maw of the starving bird. She stared fascinated, and
felt like a mother feeding her babe.

Now she had something to live for. Evening after evening
she hastened home to the solace of her ministry, till one
night the bird rose up with craning neck, its great wings
sweeping the floor—her babe no longer, but a man grown
restless for the outer world, as the strong rumour of the sea

invaded its haven. With tears she recognised the end of the companionship.

She cut the cord on its feet and felt the bird lusty in her arms. She clung to it, her face whipped with the powerful wings, and staggered to the stair-head. The evening was high, clear, and calm. 'Good-bye,' she cried, and opened her arms. Up, up, in strong flight, squawking loudly; up into the clear heaven, standing out against the opal sky. Over the Planting into the north it flew, and the monstrous sky was empty.

She returned to her room and sat in the lampless dusk, and in the silence heard the phantom hobbled feet which would never, never more crackle and scrape on the floor. She had lost her second friend.

By the sea-edge, schooled to patience, her face became sadder, her eyes quieter. The silence of the sea, the solitude of the hills were part of her being. In the summer and part of the autumn she ceased from the shore and gathered the swathes behind the mowers. Her body was strong and supple, and she could work without great fatigue for a whole day. The work was a holiday for it brought respite from solitude. Pleasant to her was the conversation at the dinner-hour in the shade of the hedges. 'It's meat an' drink to be wi' folk whiles,' she would say cheerily.

The iron of circumstance galled her soul so much now that she began to dream of eternal rest. She wondered if she would rejoin the plumber. It was the dream of a more wonderful dawn than had ever broken upon her sight across the sea. When overcome with weariness there would steal across her, like music, the thought that rest could be gained at any time in the sepulchre of cool, shadowy darkness at her feet. Sitting on a rock, her whelk-can at her side, she would gaze into the sea beneath her, watching the shimmering green. It was a place unvisited by hunger, unvexed by toil. She whispered to herself that were it not for the kindly face of the land she would go. Fixing a wistful gaze on the wide sky and its sailing clouds, the green of the valleys and the old forests, the isles and the winding beaches, and the sea itself, hung with the shadows of woods as the walls of a room with paintings, she would whisper:

'It's as white and bonny as a waen's cairryin' clothes,' and sighing, would bend to scraping again in the tangle. Penury was now disarmed. She went, accompanied by the secret thought of rest.

One morning she saw a dead man in the water beneath Barlaggan. Unafraid she dragged the body ashore; with her shawl dried the yellow-stained face, and in it wrapped the body. She found strength to be alone with the dead; and not till the policeman came that night and questioned her did she know fear. The look of the dead would not depart from her—the wet hair, the blue of the withered eyes, drained for ever of their moisture. 'As blae as a berry' they were, she told the policeman.

The following morning she stopped at sight of the Barlaggan beach, suddenly afraid of the sea. Where would *she* have gone? Only now she thought of that. It was a cold, cruel beast, this sea. How its waters had plashed in the open, raw mouth and about the grey hair matted on the temples. What a poor thing *she* would have been bobbing in by the Perch, past the Island, through the herring-boats, till she came all tangled and ragged, with her boots full of water, to the mud beneath the shops—her tippet awry, her dress torn, her breasts wounded, lying on her back, her face up to the sky. The fishermen would carry her away, shaking their heads and whispering. They would not bury her beside the plumber, but in a lonely place, with a piece of wood at her head. No, God be thankit, she hadn't done it, and without looking so much as once, turned her back upon the sea and bade it farewell for ever. She saw the corn wave on Lonend, and a flood of happiness filled her heart. She stood listening to the birds in the wood, and hated death with a great hatred, and the sea, its regent. A long-broken string in the harp was mended. Her mind bloomed like a late winter flower, and people saw on her face a new content. She overtook some children on the road beyond the 'Ghost'. She did not, as she was used, furtively steal by, but walked behind them, greedy of ear for their babble. She seemed to herself to have suffered resurrection. Her mind was smoothed and folded down out of all asperity. She believed in the compassion of God, in the kindliness of man, and made up her mind—she would open a shop. No longer would she rake on that lonely shore, beside that cruel sea.

She turned in at the door of the Good Templars' Hall. In the ante-room upon a table, in a long black coffin, lay the stranger whom the sea had brought to her feet. To-morrow at noon he was to be buried. Timidly, she stepped forward, drawing her shawl about her head, and peered. Something deep down stirred within her—a sense of the sadness and pathos which that strange still face gave to the room. The tears welled up in her eyes. She went forward on tip-toe, touched the cold brow with her hand, and closing her eyes, laid her lips upon the forehead.

With a swelling in her throat she hurried out, scuffled up to the street, knocked at the postmaster's door, and asked him if he would rent to her the shop in MacCalman's Lane. Her renunciation was complete. She had triumphed over the sea.

[from *Gillespie*, pp. 119–24]

Martha's Dance

from THE QUARRY WOOD

NAN SHEPHERD (1893–1981) wrote three novels, each one alive with poetic insight and sharp observation.

Born in West Cults, near Aberdeen, and educated at the university in the city, she taught for forty-one years at the College of Education, tended her garden, walked the hills, and accepted the world with clarity and realism. One fruit of her walks was *The Living Mountain*, a small book about her experience of the Cairngorms, which sparkles like winter light on icy rock.

In this extract from *The Quarry Wood*, the protesting Martha is carried off to stay with her grand-aunt Josephine, whose fierce singularity is central to the story.

Aunt Josephine made no overtures. She trudged leisurely in through the soft dust, her skirt trailing a little and worrying the powder of dust into fantastic patterns. If she spoke it was to herself as much as to Martha—a trickle of commentary on the drought and the heat, sublime useless ends of talk that required no answer. Martha heard them all. They settled slowly over her, and she neither acknowledged them nor shook them off. She ploughed her way stubbornly along a cart-rut, where the dust was thickest and softest and rose in fascinating puffs and clouds at the shuffle of her heavy boots. She bent her head forward and watched it smoke and seethe; and ignored everything else in the world but that and her own imagination.

But in the wood there were powers in wait for her: the troubled hush of a thousand fir-trees; a light so changed, so subdued from its own lively ardour to the dark solemnity of that which it had entered, that the child's spirit, brooding and responsive, went out from her and was liberated. In that hour was born her perception of the world's beauty.

61

The quiet generosity of the visible and tangible world sank into her mind, and with every step through the wood she felt it more closely concentrated and expressed in the gracious figure of old Mrs Leggatt. She therefore drew closer to her aunt, looking sidelong now and then into her face.

Beyond the wood they were again on dusty road, and curious little tufts of wind came *fichering* with the dust; and suddenly a steady blast was up and about, roaring out of the south-east, and the long blue west closed in on them, nearer and denser and darker, inky, then ashen, discoloured with yellow like a bruise.

'It's comin' on rainin',' said Martha; and as the first deliberate drops thumped down, she came close up to Aunt Josephine and clutched her skirt.

'We're nearly hame, ma dear, we're nearly hame,' said Aunt Josephine; and she took the child's hand firmly in hers and held back her eager pace. Thunder growled far up by the Hill o' Fare, then rumbled fiercely down-country like a loosened rock; and in a moment a frantic rain belaboured the earth. Martha tugged and ran, but Aunt Josephine had her fast and held her to the same sober step.

'It's a sair brae,' she said. 'We'll be weet whatever, an' we needna lose breath an' bravery baith. We're in nae hurry—tak yer time, tak yer time.'

They took their time. The rain was pouring from Martha's shapeless hat, her sodden frock clung to her limbs, her boots were in pulp. But Aunt Josephine had her stripped and rolled in a shawl, the fire blazing and the kettle on, before she troubled to remove her own dripping garments or noticed the puddles that spread and gathered on the kitchen floor.

Martha was already munching cake and Aunt Josephine was on her knees drying up the waters, when the sound of a voice made the child glance up to see a face thrust in and peering. A singular distorted monkey face, incredibly lined.

'It's Mary Annie,' said Miss Josephine. 'Come awa ben.'

A shrivelled little old woman came in.

She came apologetic. She had bought Miss Josephine a birthday cake and discovered too late that she had mistaken the day; and on the very birthday she had made her own uses of the cake. She had set it on the table when she had visitors to tea, for ornament merely. Now, in face of the wrong date, her conscience troubled her; and what if Jeannie should know? Jeannie was her daughter and terrible in rectitude; and Jeannie had been from home when Mrs. Mortimer had held her tea-party.

'Ye wunna tell Jeannie, Miss Josephine. Ye ken Jeannie, she's that gweed—ower-gweed for the likes o' me.'

'Hoots,' said Aunt Josephine, 'fat wad I dae tellin' Jeannie? Jeannie kens ower muckle as it is. There's nae harm dane to the cake, I'm sure, by bein' lookit at.'

Her heartiness restored Mary Annie's sense of pleasure; but she went away with no lightening of the anxiety that sat on her countenance.

Aunt Josephine had a curious belief that it was good for people to be happy in their own way: and a curious disbelief in the goodness of Jeannie.

'She's a—ay is she—' she said, and said no more.

'An' noo,' she added, looking at Martha, 'we'll just cut the new cake, for that ye're eatin's ower hard to be gweed. It's as hard's Hen'erson, an' he was that hard he reeshled whan he ran.'

She plunged a knife through the gleaming top of the cake, and served Martha with a goodly slice and some of the broken sugar.

'Yes, ma dear, he reeshled whan he ran. Did you ken that? An' the birdies'll be nane the waur o' a nimsch of cake.'

She moved about the room all the while she spoke, crumbling the old cake out at the window, sweeping the crumbs of the new together with her hand and tasting them, and breaking an end of the sugar to put in her mouth—with such a quiet serenity, so settled and debonair a mien, that the last puffs of Martha's perturbation melted away on the air.

But even in the excitement of eating iced cake, following as it did on her struggle and the long hot walk through the dust, was not prickly enough to keep her waking. Half the cake still clutched in her messy fingers, she fell asleep against Aunt Josephine's table; and Aunt Josephine, muttering, 'She's clean forfoch'en, the littlin—clean forfoch'en, that's fat she is,' put her to bed, sticky fingers and all, without more ado.

Martha awoke next morning with a sense of security. Like Mary Annie, she proceeded to be happy in her own way. That consisted at first in following Aunt Josephine everywhere about, dumbly, with grave and enquiring eyes. By and by she followed her to the open space before the door, and plucked her sleeve.

'Will I dance to you now?'

'Surely, ma dear, surely.'

She had never been taught to dance. Frock, boots, big-boned hands and limbs were clumsy, and her dancing was little more than a solemn series of ungainly hops. An intelligent observer might have been hard put to it to discover the rhythm to which she moved. A loving observer would have understood that even the worlds in their treading of the sky may sometimes move ungracefully. A young undisciplined star or so, with too much spirit for all its mastery of form . . . Aunt Josephine was a loving observer. She had never heard of cosmic measures, but she knew quite well that the force that urged the child to dance was the same that moved the sun in heaven and all the stars.

So she let her work alone and stood watching, as grave as Martha herself, and as happy.

'Lovely, ma dear, just lovely,' she said: and forgot about the tatties to pare and the dishtowels to wash before another thunder-plump came down.

[from *The Quarry Wood*, pp. 6–9 in the Canongate Classics omnibus edition, *The Grampian Quartet*]

CATHERINE CARSWELL

Highland Mary

from THE LIFE OF ROBERT BURNS

CATHERINE CARSWELL (1879–1946) was the younger
daughter of a Glasgow shipping merchant, and studied
music before becoming a journalist, first with the *Glasgow
Herald* and then the London *Observer*.

She published six books in her lifetime, leaving a
mixture of memoir and meditation, *Lying Awake*,
unfinished at her death. Edited by her son John,
this is included in Canongate Classics together with
her novel *Open the Door!*

Carswell's *Life of Robert Burns* shocked the Burns
Clubs when first published in 1930, but remains the
most vigorous and lively biography of the poet, treating
him with engaging honesty, intelligence, and zest.

In Tarbolton church the previous summer he had often
observed with interest one of the most modest and devout of
the female worshippers—so much so that for many weeks he
had neglected other afternoon houses of God to concentrate
there. She was young—not so young as Jean but a good
five years less in age than himself; her face was gentle and
steadfast; her hair, long and fine as silk, coiled up under
her woollen head-plaid, was perfectly golden. When the
minister gave out chapter and verse she was slow to find
the place in her small Bible, but once found it was followed
with attentive forefinger—all of which to Robert's way of
thinking was very 'love-inspiring.' So he had spoken with
her and discovered the reason of her extra care and slowness.
She was no Ayrshire girl, but was from the Cowal coast of the
Firth of Clyde, where they spoke the Gaelic. With pleasure
he had heard her soft, singing, delicately broken speech,
with delight had looked into her shy, sincere and amiable
eyes. He had learned her name—Mary Campbell—that her
father, once a preventive man, owned a small coaling vessel,

and that she was a dairymaid. It may have been on his recommendation that in November she left her Tarbolton place and became nurse-maid at 'the Castle' to Gavin Hamilton's new baby—his second boy, born that summer. But all through the winter and early spring Jean had been in sturdy possession, and April brought the *fama clamosa*. Even if Mary did not know before, she knew then all that was said of Robert.

She was of the retiring sort. When he asked her one day in April to meet him that evening in the ruined tower of the Abbey she refused. But on hearing from his own lips that he was deserted, that he was free, that he was crazy with a young man's longing and that he wanted a wife, she was not able to go on refusing. For she was in love. La Rochefoucauld might have added as a rider to his other observation that 'the heart, while still agitated by the remains of one passion, is also more likely to inspire passion in another than when it is entirely at rest.' Very soon Robert and Mary were meeting as often as meetings for such work-ridden creatures as themselves were possible—that is to say, every Sunday in daylight and every weekday that could be managed after dark. And because of her outlandishness and his desperation these meetings brimmed with a peculiar sweetness. Jean had been willing with the homely and hearty willingness of a young heifer. But Mary was wilder, gentler in her yielding. She was quiet, superstitious, with a delicacy of spirit and a capacity for sacrifice to which Jean would always be a stranger. She fulfilled his boyish dreams. And he had sought her out and won her, not she him. Would she marry him, he asked? Seeing him tender and sincere, she said she would. Would she also trust him? For good reasons they could not immediately celebrate their marriage. Though morally free, Robert had still to receive ecclesiastical discharge from his promise to Jean, which discharge Dr Auld would give him, he was assured, when he had stood in church for his three rebukes. Would Mary trust him? Mary would and did. During the last fortnight of April and the first fortnight of May they loved without reserve. Not even Smith shared their secret. Before May was well advanced Mary knew that in due time she would bear Robert a child.

Meeting at night beneath the still tightly closed buds of the hawthorns the lovers measured themselves against fate. They kissed and made their difficult arrangements. Mary must still trust Robert and do as he said. She could not remain in Mauchline—not till the faintest suspicion might be aroused. Term day—May the fifteenth—was near. She must give the Hamiltons immediate notice on the usual plea that her mother needed her at home to help with the younger children. She would tell her parents that she was tokened and had come home to prepare for her speedy marriage. Robert would send them a letter setting forth his honourable intentions. As soon as things were cleared for him he would come for her; or if this were prevented, she would meet him at Greenock, where she had an uncle in the carpentering line, or at Glasgow—if it was from Glasgow port he would sail. At either place they would be publicly married. They cherished the idea that they might then even sail to the Indies together. In the interval she would not be able to write to him, but he would write to her and send her the songs that welled from his heart at every thought of her.

So they made their plans, as daring and well-meaning a pair of lovers as ever kissed. But Mary was Highland. Before she went she would have Robert swear on the Holy Book itself and would herself so swear. And she would have their vows repeated across running water, so to placate the grudging powers of nature. Only thus could she travel away alone and face her parents.

Robert was the last man to deny these requests. So the jeering prophecy of Mrs Armour was fulfilled. He purported to contract another irregular union. This time he would put such awe upon the woman that she would dread faithlessness as a danger to her very soul. For himself, the more firmly he was committed the better he was pleased. Therefore on Sunday evening, the fourteenth, when Mary's little box was corded in her attic, they met under Stairaird crag at that quiet ferny place where Mauchline burn runs over a shelf of rock into Ayr river. Leaping across the narrower water Robert knelt by Mary's direction (he being less knowing than she in such procedures); and he on the further bank, she on the nearer, they joined hands under the current, thus

solemnly to pledge their troth. Then they exchanged the
Bibles each had brought. Robert's was a smart, two-volume
one, gilt-edged, and with his name, his Mason mark and the
Mossgiel address on its fly-leaves. Producing his ink-horn
and 'old stumpie,' his quill—which he was used to carry
with him for the taking down of stray song-music—he first
added Mary's name to his own in each volume, and then
he wrote on the blank pages opposite these awful words:

> On vol i—'And ye shall not swear by My Name false-
> ly—I am the Lord.—Levit. 19th chap.: 12th verse.'
> And on vol ii—'Thou shalt not forswear thyself, but
> shalt perform unto the Lord thine Oath.—Matth. 5
> Ch.: 33rd Verse.'

What he wrote in Mary's Bible for his own reminder will
never be known, but surely it was every bit as solemn and
binding. Mary was satisfied that she was truly married
according to Scots Law and the Evangel, as well as by the
rites of jealous nature. And so indeed she was, unless Robert
should choose to perjure himself, which was unthinkable.
Next day, sad but confident, she set off on her tedious
journey by cart and sail to Campbeltown in Kintyre, where
her parents were now living. And Robert, writing that night
in the rat-haunted Mossgiel parlour, his heart melting at the
thought of her, his chair balanced on its back legs, composed
the following lines—for a son of Mr Aiken's who was leaving
home for the first time:

> The sacred lowe o' weel-plac'd love,
>   Luxuriantly indulge it,
> But never tempt th' illicit rove,
>   Tho' naething should divulge it.
> I wave the quantum of the sin,
>   The hazard of concealing;
> But och! it hardens a' within,
>   And petrifies the feeling!

There was nothing of the 'illicit' in his feeling for Mary.
He was 'luxuriantly' possessive and had bounded himself
'by secret troth and honour's band.' By his own code
he was as truly married to her as if all the powers of
Church and State had tied the knot. After swinging a
little longer on the back legs of his chair and chewing

'old stumpie' he smiled and sat foursquare and wrote
further:

> If ye have made a step aside—
>   Some hap mistake o'erta'en you,
> Yet still keep up a decent pride,
>   And ne'er o'er far demean you.
> Time comes wi' kind oblivion's shade,
>   And daily darker sets it;
> And if nae mair mistakes are made,
>   The warld soon forgets it.

[from *The Life of Robert Burns*, pp. 154–8]

NANCY BRYSSON MORRISON

Taking Shelter
from THE GOWK STORM

The Gowk Storm was a Book Society Choice when first
issued in 1930, but was for a long time out of print.
NANCY BRYSSON MORRISON (1907–86) wrote more than
a dozen other books, and remained always a writer of
grace and sensibility, but The Gowk Storm is the most
passionately alive of her novels, with a unique flavour
of lucid intensity.

'Wrap yoursels up weel,' Nannie told Julia and me, 'for I
can tell frae the feel in the wind that it's the Gowk Storm
that's boding.'

We were standing in the kitchen before setting off for
Barnfingal. Nannie's face was fire-flushed as she stooped
over the girdle. It was not her usual baking-day, but Mr
Ferguson, the Balmader minister, had come to visit papa,
and visitors were as important to Nannie as they were to
us. I asked her to give me something to eat before I left and
she lifted from the girdle, with hands dusted with flour, a
pancake which was so gloriously hot I had to keep changing
it from hand to hand as I ate it.

'There is something so unlikely about snow in April,'
Julia said pensively, staring out of the little side window.

'Ay,' Nannie conceded, 'juist when the farmers are talking
o' sowing and lambing. But it's the unlikely things that
always happen in this world.'

'The poor lambs and primroses,' condoled Julia.

'It will pass if they but thole it,' Nannie said summarily,
sitting on the creepie with the bellows between her knees
and blowing the fire brighter. 'That's whit Gowk Storm
means, something o' ill chance that micht fa' to ony o' us
and that willna bide. Noo dinna dawdle on the way hame,

70

for I canna think it's juist a lesson that keeps ye so lang every aifternoon ye gang to Barnfingal.'

Fingal was discountenancing on the other side of the loch and storm brooded in the fir trees which stood out, deepened in hue, against the monotonously grey sky. Our footsteps rang on the road and a piercing north wind blew, ranging through the budding trees. It was so bleak I was glad to reach Barnfingal.

The schoolroom was a long low room built on, like an afterthought, to the dominie's house, the only two-storied building, besides Gow's Farm, in Barnfingal. All the previous schoolmasters had possessed a numerous family; and as we crossed the playground that afternoon, it struck me for the first time that our dominie must find his house a little solitary shared only by his shadow. It might have been uninhabited, for nothing could be seen through its four uncurtained windows, against which the light, distorted on the blind glass, flattened itself as though unable to enter.

Julia was restless that afternoon; perhaps Nannie's last words had disturbed her. She kept talking to us while I was having my lesson, so that the dominie, for makeweight, gave me a little longer. When he had done with me, Julia said she would like to go for a walk on the hills. He agreed readily enough, although he did say there was snow in the wind; but warnings never meant anything to Julia, and the three of us started off from the schoolroom.

Once on the hills we found the dominie was right, for the wind was so bitter and cold it seemed to whistle through one. We were glad to take shelter from it in a little hut the herd had built out of a one-time croft. It was a shadowed, mouldy place where the moor came in over the threshold. The door hung from its hinges and was too large for the hut, whose low roof had been made by stretching sticks across one another and covering them with a matting of bracken. Julia's head was on the dominie's shoulder, and the shadows of the sticks fell faintly across her face, making her look as though she were behind bars.

I was peeling the bark off a twig, and thinking how sheltered and comfortable the draughty hut was compared to outside when the door suddenly jerked open. I thought it had been flung back by a sudden squall of wind, but my heart stood still as I looked over my shoulder and saw papa standing in the doorway.

His expression of amazement when he saw who was within chilled on his face as he gazed down at us, taking in every detail. I felt the paralysing sense of misgiving that I never outgrew and which always took hold of me when I saw his eyes narrow and his mouth compress. We rose to our feet, forgetting in our troubled haste that the roof was so low. He voiced no comment, for he was accompanied by Mr Ferguson, but he stood, upright and withdrawn, everything about him, from his thin nose to his alienating silence, making his displeasure felt more acutely than words.

Julia betrayed none of the disquietude she must have felt, only her face perhaps became a little flushed. But she introduced the dominie to Mr Ferguson with the same composure she would have shown had we met him in a drawing-room. The dominie, taken at a disadvantage, was ill at ease and became remote and silent as papa, while Julia conversed with Mr Ferguson with all her rallying, disarming charm.

''Pon my soul, 'pon my soul,' he said with the diffuseness of a breathless man, 'we didn't think to find your sanctuary inhabited, did we, William? Don't let us chase you away, Miss Lockhart. We're on our way to see the Roman encampment, but I said to your father if he didn't find me a place where I could draw breath without being winded, I would expire.'

I do not think he had seen into the hut when Julia's head was on the dominie's shoulder, for he was a little behind papa, but the meeting in itself was untoward and he must have sensed tension from papa's protracted icy silence and the dominie's stiffness. An ardent fisherman, however, who pursued his hobby from morning to night in the face of his congregation's united disapproval, he was accustomed to shutting his eyes to the obvious. He now rose to the occasion with abandon, ostentatiously overlooking anything amiss to the extent of shaking hands warmly with Julia although he was seeing her again within the hour.

There was silence between us as we walked away until we

were well out of earshot of the hut when Julia, waves of colour breaking over her face, turned to the dominie and said:

'Well, you were not very helpful, were you?'

'I am sorry,' he returned, 'but I could think of nothing to say.'

'It was not only that you stood and said nothing,' she retorted, swallowing, 'but, upon my word, you might have been in league with papa.'

'It was a very trying situation for your father,' he pointed out.

'Trying situation for papa!' she exclaimed angrily as a few flakes of snow began to fall uncertainly. 'Trying situation for papa! And do you think it was a pleasant and comfortable situation for me?—particularly when I knew that papa had wanted me expressly to help to entertain Mr Ferguson this afternoon, and I had made some trifling excuse because I wanted to be with you. Trying for papa! I assure you it is entirely your fault that a situation so trying for papa arose in the first place.' He attempted to speak but she would brook no interruption. 'It is because of you our meetings are secretive and stolen, is it not? I do not think you will deny that. Do you intend they should always be so? I, for one, despise and abominate concealment: there would be need of none of it once you came openly to the manse—'

'You know your father would never permit that,' he said. 'There is the difference in our religions for one thing.'

'And are we any nearer bridging that difficulty now than we were six months ago?' she demanded. 'Has a Catholic never married a Protestant before?'

There was a pause, a waiting pause which, for me, prolonged itself unbearably, although I do not think Julia noticed it, for she was arranging her own disordered thoughts. But as I walked beside the dominie through the snow that was now whirling thickly down, I found myself wondering if he had made himself believe that the difference in their religion stayed him from all possible action. Even then I realised that he confessed, never declared, his love, and was so afraid of happiness he had to do penance for any that came his way.

'I wonder if another thing has struck you,' Julia pursued

hotly, 'and that is that papa will demand an explanation whenever Mr Ferguson leaves to-night.'

I felt her words pulled at him, that she was pinning him down, against his will, with her decision.

'I should have known,' he cried out, almost in agony, 'I should have known this would happen—it is all my fault.'

[from *The Gowk Storm*, pp. 63–7]

NEIL M. GUNN

A Leaf in the Wind
from SUN CIRCLE

NEIL M. GUNN (1891–1973) was born in Dunbeath, Caithness, the seventh of nine children. His father was a locally renowned fishing skipper, but his mother wanted her sons to avoid the treacherous sea and gain education in the world beyond. Gunn spent twenty-six years in the excise service, travelling all over the Highlands before settling as officer attached to an Inverness distillery. In 1937 he resigned to write full-time.

Gunn's twenty-one novels combine emotional intensity and intellectual penetration to a degree that arouses strong response, for or against, and reach a depth and force rare in the literature of any country.

Sun Circle, his fourth novel, explores with passionate insight the Viking invasion of his native Caithness.

Glancing inside, he saw the priest's kneeling body doubled over a stool. The head had fallen forward and the hands hung down to the ground, like a body that death had visited in prayer.

Aniel went into the hut; he touched the body, at the same time speaking aloud to give himself courage. The body stirred, and presently Molrua was blinking upward from his knees. 'What is it, my son?' He arose.

'The Northmen have landed and defeated us. My father and Drust and a great number have been slain. The Northmen are coming up the glen now. They will be here at once.'

Aniel spoke quickly and Molrua gazed steadfastly at him, but with the light that only half sees the outward vision.

Aniel urged him restlessly.

'I fell asleep,' said Molrua. 'I set myself to watch and pray, but I fell asleep.' His voice was quiet and gentle; there was in it a condemnation so complete that it was passionless; there was nothing that Molrua could add to his self-knowledge, nothing that man could not fail in. He smiled.

A cold shiver rayed from the nape of Aniel's neck. 'Come—at once,' he stuttered.

'So you ran to save me?' The smile caught Aniel; the eyes deepened. Aniel grew suddenly warm and awkward in the light of that humility.

'There is time yet—if we hurry.'

'God bless you, my son.' He laid a hand on Aniel's head. 'You will now save yourself. Go you.'

'Won't you come, Father?'

They went out at the door. The morning was bright with the early sun, the wind was fresh and cool, a lark sang in a sky whose blue was half veiled here and there in wisps of drawn cloud. It was a lovely morning, and the wind that cleansed was also bringing—what was it, this faint haze from the sea, this scent of . . . smoke . . . fire? Fire! It was fire! And that was a shout. Again. Again.

'They are coming, Father!'

Molrua turned towards the sea whose far horizon he could just see. Yes, they were coming. And even as they watched, three Northmen appeared over the abrupt rise in the ground beyond the meadow-flat in front of them.

'There they are!' cried Aniel under his breath, backing away at once. 'Come on!' and he slid over the inland brow of the knoll, raced down its side, and made for the Tower.

Molrua appeared not to have heard him, so concentrated was his gaze. The three Northmen, with their peaked helmets, round bodies, and busked active legs, had an odd air of unreality. As they came over the rise they paused, looking at what lay before them, then began to move about uncertainly, facing one way and then another. At last one of them, his back to Molrua, shouted and waved his sword. The other two did the same thing. Clearly they had discovered the true way and were calling their comrades.

Under the morning, it was a strange thing to see men so behave. Their limbs and their weapons stirred like the legs of great spiders. They were beings not of this world, and on the rim of it they moved in all the excitement of discovery.

Deadly and voracious they were; the prospect of death their excitement, and its reality their food. Strange to watch their dark antics in the fresh light of so clear a morning. Strange that these creatures should be God's creatures, too. Deep the mystery of God. Deep Thy mystery, O God.

Molrua turned and went into his hut. His legs were trembling a little and so he sat down on the stool over which, as he yet prayed, he had fallen asleep. Seated, he looked before him, his hands limp against the wood.

. . .

Molrua went out at the door, and before him at a few paces a Northman was standing on the grassy crest. He looked fixedly at Molrua, his knuckles standing out upon the shaft of his axe. A cut on his left temple dropped a red thread to the eyebrow. The lips were hard against the teeth.

Molrua felt the whiteness about him more than ever, as though Someone were now coming in upon his right hand. He had no fear, and as his eyes glimmered he raised his open hand. This action released the Northman. Molrua did not stir, and so the axe, descending, severed the lips while they were still blessing.

Retrieving his axe, the Northman glanced about him. He had an uneasy feeling of other presences. The strange look on the man's face had strung up all his muscles so that he had had to come at him quickly, urged from within. He eyed the gaping door of the little round house and went to it quickly. But he was in only for a moment when he glanced out again and from side to side. Then he ransacked the interior, tearing down, and kicking over and breaking a jar and spilling the water upon his feet. In that simple dwelling the most valuable thing was the hide case with its copy of the Gospels. There was neither gold nor silver. Even the carved head of the bachall or staff was innocent of metal ornament.

At the door again, the Northman glanced about him, glanced at the vellum pages of the scriptures in his hands and threw them from him. It was altogether a queer place this, and quite possibly he had killed one of the terrible magicians who offered up sacrifices with black rites.

He strode away, but at the crest had to look over his shoulder. There was no one there, nothing but the dead body and a leaf of that which he had thrown from him moving in the wind.

[from *Sun Circle*, pp. 125–33]

The Preacher and the Tinks

from CLOUD HOWE

JAMES LESLIE MITCHELL (1901–35), who also wrote
under the name Lewis Grassic Gibbon, was born and
raised in the North-East of Scotland, and after service
in the RAF became in 1928 a full-time writer, driven
by financial pressure to produce nine books in six years.
He died from a perforated ulcer at thirty-four. The *Scots
Quair* trilogy has long been accepted as a landmark in
Scottish twentieth-century literature both for its scope
and its use of language. *Cloud Howe*, the second book in
the series, deals with the marriage of the widowed Chris
Tavendale (née Guthrie) and the tormented radical minister Robert Colquhoun, condemned to inhabit the town
of Segget, which is described here with Gibbon's characteristic verve and irony in all its quarrelsome vigour.

And next Sabbath MacDougall Brown, the postmaster,
came down to the Square and preached on stealing, right
godly-like, and you'd never have thought that him and his
wife stayed up of a night sanding the sugar and watering
the paraffin—or so folk said, but they tell such lies. He
was maybe fifty years old, MacDougall, a singer as well
as a preacher, i'faith! though some said his voice was the
kind of a thing better suited to slicing a cheese. During the
War he had fair been a patriot, he hadn't fought, but losh!
how he'd sung! In the first bit concert held in the War he
sang Tipperary to the Segget folk, with his face all shining
like a ham on the fry, and he sang it right well till he got
to the bit where the song has to say that his heart's right
there. And faith, MacDougall got things a bit mixed, he
clapped down his hand the wrong side of his wame; and
Ake Ogilvie that sat in the front of the hall gave a coarse
snicker and syne everybody laughed; and MacDougall had
never forgiven Ake that. But he got on well with his post-office

place, Johnnie his son was a bit of a fool and MacDougall
sent him to take round the letters, it cost him little with
a son that was daft and MacDougall kept the cash for
himself. Forbye young Jock he'd two daughters as well, the
eldest, Cis, was bonny and trig, with a grave, douce face,
she went to the College but she wasn't proud, a fine bit
queen, and all Segget liked her.

Well, MacDougall had a special religion of his own, he
wasn't Old Kirk and he wasn't of the Frees, he wasn't even
an Episcopalian, but Salvation Army, or as near as damn it.
He went on a Sabbath morn to the Square and preached there
under the lee of the angel, that the road to heaven was the way
he said. He'd made two-three converts in his years in Segget,
they'd stand up and say what the Lord had done, how before
they'd met Him they were lost, ruined souls: but now God
had made them into new men. And faith! you would think,
if that was the case, the Lord's handiwork was failing, like
everything else.

Well, that Sunday after the row at Smithie's, he was there
at his stance where the angel stood, MacDougall himself with
his flat, bald head, and beside him his mistress, a meikle
great sumph, she came from the south and she mouthed
her words broad as an elephant's behind, said Ake Ogilvie.
She thought little of Cis, that was clever and bonny, but a
lot of her youngest, the quean called Mabel—by all but her
mother, she called her May-bull. Well, they both were there,
and the daftie Jock, gleying, and slavering up at the angel,
and a two-three more, the gardener Grant and Newlands
the stationy, them and their wives; with the angel above
with her night-gown drawn back, right handy-like, in case
it might rap against the bald pow of MacDougall Brown.
Mistress Brown opened up the harmonica they'd brought,
it groaned and spluttered and gave a bit hoast, syne they
started the singing of their unco hymns, Newlands burring
away in his boots and MacDougall slicing the words like
cheese.

Syne MacDougall started to preach about stealing, with
a verse from Leviticus for the text, though the case of old
Smithie had supplied the cause; and they started singing
another bit hymn, all about being washed in the Blood of

the Lamb, the Lamb being Jesus Christ, said MacDougall, he was awful fond of hymns full of blood, though he'd turned as white as a sheet the time Dite Peat had come over to kill his pig, and asked MacDougall to hold the beast down.

Well, they were getting on fine and bloody, and having fairly a splash in the gore, when MacDougall noticed there was something wrong, the words all to hell, he couldn't make it out. Syne his mistress noticed and screwed round her head, and she said *What is 't?* and saw MacDougall, red as rhubarb, he'd stopped his singing. The rest of them had to do the same, for a drove of the spinners had come in about, with that tink Jock Cronin at their head, as usual, they were singing up fast and fair drowning MacDougall, a coarse-like mocking at MacDougall's hymn:

WHITER than—the whitewash on the wall!
WHITER than—the whitewash on the wall!
Oh—WASH me in the water
Where you washed your dirty daughter,
And I shall be whiter than the whitewash on the wall!

MacDougall waited until they had stopped, then he cried to Cronin *Have you no respect—you, John Cronin—for the Lord's Day at all?* And the tink said, *Damn the bit; nor have you.* And MacDougall nearly burst to hear that, he'd lived by the Bible all his life. And John Cronin said *You believe all that's in it?* and MacDougall Brown said, *Ay, I have faith.* But Cronin had fairly got him trapped now, he said *Well, it says in the Bible that if you've got faith you can move a mountain. That'll be proof. Move back the Mounth there in front of our eyes!*

The spinners with him, a lot of tink brutes, all brayed up then. *Ay, come on, MacDougall! Move a mountain—you're used to move sand!* MacDougall habbered redder than ever, then he cried *We'll now sing Rock of Ages.* Jock Cronin cried *Where's the rock of your faith?* and as soon as MacDougall and his converts began the spinners sang up their song as before, about being whiter than the whitewash on the wall, and about MacDougall's dirty daughter; and such a noise was never heard before in the Sabbath Square of Segget.

Old Leslie came by and he heard the noise, and he knew

MacDougall and was right sorry for him. But when he came over and tried to interfere, Jock Cronin cried *Christ, here's Ananias!* And old Leslie walked away, fair in a rage, and went up to the Manse to complain about them.

He arrived there just after the morning service, the minister new back, and dinner-time done. And old Leslie said 'twas Infernal, just, the way that they treated a man nowadays. In his young days if a loon like that Cronin had miscalled a man he'd have been ta'en out and libbed. Ay, he minded when he was a loon up in Garvock—

But the new minister rose up and said *Well, I'll hear that again, I've no time to waste,* with a look as black as though he could kill you. And afore old Leslie knew well what had happened he was out on the doorstep and heard the door bang.

[from *Cloud Howe*, pp. 48–51 in the Canongate Classics edition of the trilogy, *A Scots Quair*]

Elizabeth and Elise

from IMAGINED CORNERS

WILLA MUIR (1890–1970) gained a first-class Honours degree at the University of St. Andrews in 1910, before going on to study Educational Psychology and become first a lecturer and then Vice-Principal of a London Training College. She married the poet Edwin Muir in 1919, and the couple travelled Europe, translating plays and novels from the German.

She published five books of her own, two of them novels, of which *Imagined Corners* emerges as one of the most distinctive Scottish books of the 1930s.

The passage quoted describes the first meeting between Elizabeth Shand, unhappily married in the small town of Calderwick, and that other Elizabeth Shand, now known as Elise, who years before scandalously ran off with a German, and returns to confront her upbringing.

The eye sees what it looks for, and Elizabeth was looking for her other self. Had it been a man whose arrival she was expecting with so much interest she would have been embarrassed by that interest; had it been a man who now came into the room she would have been afraid of her own emotion; but since Elise was a woman Elizabeth did not know that she actually fell in love with her at first sight.

Elise, cool and sparkling, noted that it was Mabel who showed off Hector, and that it was left to John to bring forward the shy, large, awkward creature who called herself Elizabeth Shand. She examined her namesake with a satirical eye: one of these earnest women who don't know how to do their hair, she decided, and turned to Hector again with unconcealed surprise.

'I should have guessed you were a brother of mine even if I had met you at the bottom of the sea.'

She stared at him frankly.

'What a curious experience it is to meet someone so like oneself!'

'You're not very like each other, really,' put in John.

'Oh, but I think they are,' cried Mabel.

'Well,' said Elise, 'it takes the conceit out of me to find that I am merely a family type instead of an original model.'

But even as she said this she was discovering that Hector's mouth was different from hers: the lips were less finely turned, and opened over slightly irregular teeth: it was a larger mouth, too, a less discriminating mouth, a weaker mouth than hers.

'You're both black Shands,' said John. 'I went through all the family papers and albums when our father died, and I found that it was our father's grandmother on his father's side who was the first of that type in the family. But it's only a general family resemblance.'

'Black Shands?' commented Elise. 'I suppose Black Sheep is what you really mean, John?'

'How did you guess it, Elise? Hector is a double-dyed black sheep.'

Mabel's playful, provocative tone perfectly underlined her meaning, which was further emphasized by the hand she laid on Hector's shoulder. She wanted to let Elise see that she, too, had a way with men. Hector, who was a little taken aback by the elegance of his half-sister, welcomed Mabel's gambit with relief, and followed it up so thoroughly that the room was presently dominated by their brisk exchange of invective, which was kept up even after they were all seated at table.

Elise was half exasperated and half amused. She thought that they were both 'showing off' before her. How was the wife taking it? she wondered, and stole a glance at her. Elizabeth Shand's eyes were cast down: it was impossible to tell from her face what her feelings were. A real Scottish face, Elise thought, all nose and cheek-bones: the black Shands were certainly of an entirely different type. 'That great-grandmother of ours,' she said to John, 'the first black Shand, was she a Scot, do you know?'

Her eyes were still resting absently on the face of the other Elizabeth, as if it were merely an exhibit in a museum of

Scottish faces, but she was startled by the change which flitted over it when she began to speak. The girl lifted her eyes as if with an effort, as if a weight had been holding her eyelids down, and looked straight across the table at her. Elise almost jumped: the eyes were so intensely alive, the expression in them so completely altered the whole face. She felt unexpectedly embarrassed, as if she had been caught prying.

[from *Imagined Corners*, pp. 165–7, in the Canongate Classics omnibus edition, *Imagined Selves*]

In the Cellar

from THE EARLY LIFE OF JAMES MCBEY

JAMES MCBEY (1883–1959) made his reputation as an etcher, and served as official artist in the First World War. He spent the last years of his life in North Africa, an American citizen.

After the Second War McBey began his memoirs with a stark and vivid account of his harsh early life but abandoned the book unfinished. It remained unpublished until 1977. He describes unflinchingly in its pages his fanatical self-educative zeal while living with a thrawn, bitter, blind and loveless mother and an idiosyncratic grandmother, working by day in an Aberdeen bank and by night in a cold studio. The extract here describes his mother's death with a bleak honesty which makes the hair rise on the back of the neck. *The Early Life of James McBey* is a minor masterpiece which lives in the reader's mind like a memory of his (or her) own.

One night—the 11th of December 1906—I worked later than usual. From pencil sketches I was painting in a small figure of an old woman gathering driftwood on the beach at Catterline. It gave me a lot of trouble and I had to wipe it out several times. I became so engrossed that I lost count of time and stopped only when my hands became too cold to hold the brush. It was nearly 9.30 p.m. when I reached home. Both my grandmother and Annie had gone to bed.

At 2.30 a.m. I was awakened by my grandmother shaking my shoulder. In the light of the candle which she carried her face had a perplexed look.

'Annie is not in her bed.'

Knowing that Annie often spent night hours sitting muffled up in the parlour I replied,

'She is probably in the parlour.'

'No, I have looked there.'

'Then where could she be? She could not have gone out alone. We must just search everywhere we can think of.'

I opened the door to the stairs and listened. All was quiet. There was only one other place I could think of—a very unlikely one.

'She may have gone to the cellar for some reason and tripped over something. I'll go down and look.'

My grandmother replied, 'I think I'll come with you.'

'All right, but it's bitterly cold.'

Together we went down slowly and softly and apprehensively, I holding the candlestick. We reached the basement and turned into the open space in front of the cellar doors.

There, in the dim light cast by my candle, stood Annie fully clothed. Behind me my grandmother called gently, 'Why are you down here in the cold?' Suddenly the hairs of my body stood up. I saw that Annie's feet were not touching the ground.

I turned in front of my grandmother.

'Come back upstairs. I must get my knife.'

She looked at me for a moment perplexed before her eyes dilated. She turned without a word. I helped her upstairs, made her sit down, forbad her to move, and got my pocket knife.

Quickly I tiptoed back to the basement and set my candlestick on the floor. It took all my courage to approach the silent figure turning so slightly. I reached up and cut the two cords above her head. She fell heavily at my feet. With difficulty I undid the noose almost embedded in her neck, my fingers fumbled so. Her head and hands were quite cold.

I hurried upstairs making no noise as I was barefooted. My grandmother was exactly as I had left her. I lit a lamp. I told her I was going to fetch a doctor, to put on warm clothes and not to leave the room or make any noise. She appeared dazed but nodded understanding. I was fearful that one of the other tenants sleeping all round us would get to know anything of this night's happenings.

Quietly I got my cycle downstairs. I knew no doctor,

but I cycled towards Bon-accord Square on the railing of which were many doctors' brass plates. I rang the bell of the first one—a Dr Wyness. After what seemed an interminable wait he opened the door, and took me into his waiting-room.

'What can I do for you?'

'My mother (it was with a conscious effort I used those two words) has hanged herself at 42 Union Grove. Will you come with me?'

'If she has hanged herself, I can do nothing. You must go to the police.'

He showed me out, and I mounted my cycle and sped down silent Union Street.

A black cat darting across the street ran right underneath my forewheel, throwing me off. Fortunately my cycle was not twisted. The police station was, to my intense relief, partially open.

I had never been inside a police station. I knew not what to expect and certainly did not anticipate sympathy. Now, in front of a uniformed official at a desk, I found myself very calm. Guardedly I said, 'I have to report a suicide.' He looked searchingly at me for a few seconds then without a word went to another room and returned accompanied by another officer.

'This is Inspector Wilson. He will take charge of the case. Please sit down and answer his questions.' The inspector wrote down my replies on a sheet of paper which they handed me to sign. The officer then said, 'You have a cycle outside. The inspector will go with you.'

Side by side, without a word being spoken, the inspector and I cycled up to Union Grove.

'Is the body still in the basement?'

'Yes, I'll show you where. Would you come as quietly as possible?'

He followed close behind me to the basement, lighting the way with his bull's-eye lantern.

He flashed his light all around and on Annie's body. He scrutinised closely the deep groove around her neck, then asked, 'Where is the rope?' An end of rope was projecting from beneath her dress. This I handed to him.

He examined it closely. Instantly he was all suspicion, and drew himself up.

'This rope is not cut.'

'Then there must be another piece somewhere.'

He turned his lantern and there behind him lay the piece which had formed the noose. This and the other cut piece which still hung from the beam of the low ceiling he examined very closely.

'I'll take those pieces of rope. Do any of your neighbours know what has happened?'

'No one, so far.'

'All right. You help me and we'll carry the body upstairs.'

Between us we carried Annie to where my grandmother was seated, waiting, and laid her body gently on the floor of the parlour. He asked my grandmother the same questions as he had asked me at the police station. She replied with a calmness and a lucidity which must have impressed him. I asked him anxiously, 'Will all this be in the press?'

'I shall do my best to prevent it. There is no public inquest but you will have to be examined by the Procurator Fiscal. I will hide the charge book for a few days and at the headquarters we'll say to the reporters it has been mislaid. Once several days pass it will be stale news and they will not print anything about it. Take your grandmother back to the kitchen. I'll put things as straight as I can before it is too late.'

No words that I knew could have expressed the gratitude I felt towards Inspector Wilson.

[from *The Early Life of James McBey*, pp. 64–7]

ERIC LINKLATER

The Gift of Courage
from PRIVATE ANGELO

ERIC LINKLATER (1899–1974) admired the military
virtues, yet in *Private Angelo* wrote with anarchistic
gusto the 'Good Soldier Schweik' of his generation.

Born in Penarth, but an Orkneyman by lineage and
inclination, Linklater spent a lifetime as a professional
writer of style and elegance who never wrote a clumsy
paragraph. The passage quoted opens *Private Angelo* in
that tone of ironic relish which he sustains throughout.

'The trouble with you, Angelo,' said the Count severely, 'is
that you lack the *dono di coraggio.*'

'That is perfectly true,' said Angelo, 'but am I to blame?
Courage is a gift indeed, a great and splendid gift, and it is idle
to pretend that any ordinary person can insist on receiving
it; or go and buy it in the Black Market. We who have not
been given the *dono di corragio* suffer deeply, I assure you.
We suffer so much, every day of our lives, that if there were
any justice in the world we should receive sympathy, not
reproof.'

With the back of his hand he rubbed a tear from his
cheek, and turned away to look through the tall window
at the splendid view of Rome on which it opened. In the
westering sun the walls of the buildings were the colour of
ripe peaches; the domes of several churches rose serenely,
firmly round and steeply nippled like the unimpaired and
several breasts of a Great Mother whose innumerable offspring, too weak to drain them, had even lacked sufficient
appetite to use them much; while in half a dozen places,
within easy reach of sight, Victory in a four-horsed chariot
drove superbly through the golden air. Soft green foliage
clothed the river-bank, and somewhere a military band
was playing a gallant march. How beautiful was Rome,
how beautiful all the land of Italy!

Sitting behind his handsome large table—inlaid with intricately patterned brass about its flanks and furnished with a brass inkstand as big as a couple of flower-pots, with a statuette in bronze of the Wolf and the Twins, and a signed photograph of the Duce—seated in state though he was, the Count felt a softening of his heart, and his hands which had lain flat and severe upon the table half-rose, half-turned their palms, in a little gesture of understanding and sympathy; a gesture like the prelude to a softly acquiescent shrug. Angelo was a good-looking boy. True, he was very dirty, his ill-made uniform was sweat-stained and caked with dust, his left knee showed through a long rent in his breeches, his right boot was tied with string to keep a loose sole in position, and he stank a little; but his black hair curled and the bones of his face were as comely as if Donatello in his prime had carved them; he had eyes like his mother's, and in his voice the echoes rose and fell of hers.

With the fingers of his left hand the Count played a small tune upon the table and thought of Angelo's mother when she was seventeen. His estate of Pontefiore, in the Tuscan hills between Siena and Florence, had always been renowned for the prettiness of its peasant-girls and the excellence of its wine, but in a year when the vintage was better than anyone could remember, and the girls—or so it seemed to him, in the flush of his own youth—were more enticing than ever before, Angelo's mother had stolen all the light of the sky and left in shadow every other prospect of pleasure. Her lips and her long fingers and the suppleness of her waist! The round of her hips and the white of her knees when she stooped with a lifting skirt over the washing-trough with the women and the other girls; and then, when she turned to speak to him, the darkness and the laughter in her eyes! And how short, how tragically brief, had been their time together.

Desolation like a sudden storm enclosed him in its hail and darkness when he thought of those vanished years. He, like Angelo, was now in need of sympathy, and for a moment his impulse was to rise, embrace him, and let their tears flow in a common stream of sorrow.

But as he moved, restless in his chair, his glance encountered the Duce's portrait: the autograph, the massive jaw, and the unyielding mouth. Though the Duce had lately been dismissed from his high office, and his Grand Council dissolved, the Count still kept the portrait on his table, for it was signed *Your friend Mussolini*, and he prided himself on loyalty. How often had those piercing eyes inspired him! They inspired him still, and with an effort, with reluctance, he dismissed his tender thoughts. Stiffening his muscles and sitting bolt upright, he cast out sadness like a recognized traitor, and instead of tears forced into his eyes the atrabilious gleam of the eyes in the photograph. Not only was he Count of Pontefiore, Angelo's patron and once the lover of his dead mother; he was also Commanding Officer of the 914th Regiment of Tuscan Infantry, the Sucklings of the Wolf. He was Angelo's Colonel, and when he spoke it was in a colonel's voice.

'You are a soldier and it is your duty to be courageous,' he said loudly. 'The illustrious regiment in which you have had the honour to serve, and I the honour to command, is even now fighting with the most glorious courage in Calabria. By this time, perhaps, your comrades have slaughtered the last of the English invaders or driven them into the sea. And you, you alone deserting and disgracing them, have run away! You have run all the way from Reggio to Rome!'

'The last time I saw my comrades,' said Angelo, 'they were all running away. I looked over my shoulder once or twice, and they were running as hard as they could. But none of them was so swift and determined as I, and therefore I am the first to arrive. But if you will have a little patience, I am sure that you will presently see your whole regiment here.'

'Silence!' cried the Count. 'No one in my presence shall ever deny, or even dispute, the indomitable valour of my gallant men!'

He struck with an ivory ruler the gleaming surface of the table, and then, frowning a little, leaned forward and asked, 'Is it really as bad as that?'

'Quite as bad,' said Angelo. 'It has taken us a long time to lose the war, but thank heaven we have lost it at last, and there is no use in denying it.'

'It is treason to say that.'

'It is common sense.'

'You are still a soldier,' said the Count, 'and you have no right to talk about common sense. You are subject to military law, and since by your own confession you are guilty of cowardice and desertion—well, my friend, you know the penalty for that?'

'Death,' said Angelo in a gloomy voice.

'If I do my duty, you will certainly be shot.'

'The English have been trying to shoot me for the last three years. In Cyrenaica I had the greatest difficulty in avoiding their bombs and bullets and shells. I had to run hundreds of miles to escape being killed. And now, after three years of that sort of thing, I come to see you, my patron and Commanding Officer, and almost the first thing you say is that you too want to murder me. Is there no difference at all between friend and foe?'

'There is a great deal of difference,' said the Count, 'but a soldier's duty is the same wherever you go.'

'It is, however, only a very good soldier who always does his duty.'

'That is worth bearing in mind,' said the Count thoughtfully. 'I am not eager, you must realize, to have you shot, for it would create an awkward precedent if, as you say, my whole regiment is now on its way to Rome. And yet, if I were openly to condone your cowardice, and wholly ignore the fact of your desertion, I should bring myself down to your level. I should stand shoulder to shoulder with you in dishonour.'

'It would be a new experience for you,' said Angelo. 'During three years of war you have never stood shoulder to shoulder with me or with any of your men.'

[from *Private Angelo*, pp. 1–4]

Kirstie's Funeral

from FERGUS LAMONT

ROBIN JENKINS was born in 1912 in Cambuslang, and brought up in Lanarkshire. He spent some years as a schoolteacher in Scotland, and from 1957 to 1968 taught abroad. He has, to date, published over twenty books, all with a characteristic tone of dry compassion.

Jenkins has never been fully appreciated in his native country; perhaps because his wry irony acts as a disguise to a deep abiding concern with the nature of goodness.

The passage quoted here from *Fergus Lamont* depicts the end of Fergus's sole experience of fulfilment, living in the Highlands with Kirstie, whose invincible innocence soothes his prickly spirit.

We did not deliberately plan, Mairi, Dugald, and I, a small private funeral: we just took it for granted that in this, as in everything else for the past ten years, we would be left to get on with it ourselves. With us independence had long since passed from a principle into a habit.

To satisfy the law, a doctor was needed to certify death. One was summoned with great difficulty. He came next day, Sunday, grumbling at having had to walk for miles in pouring rain. He asked for a dram before he as much as glanced at Kirstie in the bed.

That Sunday was a long wet dreich sad day.

The doctor was a cheerful, white-haired old man, semi-retired. 'Must have been her heart,' he said, as he signed. 'Famous for her strength, wasn't she? Often happens. Knew a caber-tosser once. Legs like cabers. One day there he was tossing away among the best down at the Cowal Games, and two days later he was gone. Went out like that.' He snapped his fingers. 'Bonny woman too,' he added, with a last look at Kirstie. 'I didn't know that. Well, I'll let Donald McVicar the undertaker know and he'll either come out himself or more likely send somebody for like me he's a bit shaky on the pins for a brute of a walk like that.'

'There will be no need for Mr McVicar's services,' I said. 'We shall manage.'

He had been giving me some odd looks. I was dressed in my best kilt and jacket, and was wearing my MC ribbon and medal. I felt that Kirstie would have wanted me to.

'Suit yourselves,' he said, giving me the oddest look yet. 'Like everybody else Donald's always on the look-out for business, but he might not be sorry to miss this one, on the edge of the civilised world. Were you thinking of making a coffin out of driftwood?'

'Why not?' I said. 'She gathered a lot of it in her lifetime.'

Mairi took me aside. 'I should have told you this before, Fergus,' she whispered. 'Kirstie mentioned once before that she would like a nice coffin. I doubt if you and Dugald could make one out of driftwood that would have pleased her.'

John Lamont, expert carpenter, could have, I almost said. What I did say, humbly, was: 'I'd like her to have what she wanted.'

'She also wanted a minister to take the service at the graveside.'

'That,' interposed the doctor, cheerfully, 'might not be so easy. I doubt if there is a man of God throughout the islands willing to stand up in public and send her off into eternity with his and the Lord's blessing. I mean, she wasn't married to you, was she? I understand you've got a wife living somewhere. No business of mine, but then I'm not a man of God.'

'I've been a bit worried about that,' said Mairi.

I had forgotten that, since Kirstie had been living with me in what the ministers would call a state of adultery they would hardly think her death an occasion for forgiveness.

'Bastards,' I said, bitterly.

'Well no,' said the doctor, reasonably. 'You really can't blame them. You broke their rules. So did she. If one of them was to let a fit of pure Christianity get the better of him the Lord might be pleased, but I'm damned sure his congregation and colleagues wouldn't.'

'You'd have thought,' said Mairi, with a sigh, 'that the War would have made us all a bit more tolerant.'

The doctor poured himself another dram. 'Ah, you're presupposing, Mrs McLeod, that tolerance is in itself a good thing. Not many people really believe that. Most of us are prepared to tolerate only what we understand and approve of.'

I walked with him most of the way to the road-end where his motor-car was waiting. There was little wind, but the rain was steady. We did not speak much. Every stone on that track reminded me of Kirstie, and the doctor kept damning them for bruising his feet and making him stumble.

So Kirstie had her nice coffin, made by craftsmen in Glasgow, and delivered to us by two of McVicar's henchmen. It was of polished oak, lined with white satin, and adorned with golden-coloured tassels. In it Kirstie looked like the abbess of some great convent. She should have been lying in state in a vaulted hall, with nuns praying round her.

Young Hector refused to look at her. He would not even go into the back room where the coffin lay on our kitchen table. Nor would Laddie, our collie, which raised its head and howled at intervals of half an hour.

No one sympathised with Hector more than I, who had refused to look into my mother's coffin.

Ailie was bolder. She gazed so long that her mother had to tell her to come away.

'*Is* it Kirstie?' asked Ailie, hours afterwards.

We knew what she meant. It was hard for us who had seen her spread dung and gut fish and scratch her oxters to believe that this woman with the noble, austere face had once been our Kirstie. It was hardest for me, who had slept with her.

We had loved her, but we had not valued her as much as we should.

'Don't blame yourself, Fergus,' said Mairi, weeping in my arms.

I was weeping too. 'But we laughed at her sometimes.'

'Well, why shouldn't we? She didn't mind. I think we loved her most when we were laughing at her. Well, I did, anyway. I don't know about you and Dugald and Hector. I do know about Ailie, though.'

I left it to Dugald to try and find a willing clergyman. He did not succeed. Perhaps he might have if he had had months, but he had only three days, and they included Sunday, a day when in those parts it was not possible to buy a loaf of bread far less persuade Calvinist ministers to put pity before dogma. In any case, Dugald, his own morality Deuteronomical, could not have been a very persuasive envoy.

If nobody minded, he said, and if nobody expected too much, he would himself read a passage out of the Bible at the graveside. After all, there would only be ourselves present.

Hector offered to play on his bagpipes some of the tunes Kirstie had taught him. He wasn't a very good player yet, he admitted, but Kirstie hadn't minded his mistakes.

There was the grave to dig in the old kirkyard, where the ground was stony. Dugald and I found it hard work in the rain, requiring more skill than we had thought. He kept forgetting, and remarked more than once that if we had had Kirstie to help we'd have got it done a good deal quicker.

Hector walked up and down over the old flat gravestones, practising. He tried hard but he did make many mistakes.

Mairi and Ailie brought tea and pieces. We sat in the broken church and had a sad picnic. Still forgetful, Dugald chucked away a crust—since he was five, he muttered, he'd hated black crusts; but before we had time to rebuke him for his sacrilege an attendant gull pounced on it.

We kept assuring one another that though it would not be the most expert of funerals Kirstie wouldn't have minded.

[from *Fergus Lamont*, pp. 298–301]

DAVID THOMSON

'I do count them, Sean'

from THE PEOPLE OF THE SEA

DAVID THOMSON (1914–88) gained the McVitie's prize in
1987 for his memoir of growing up in Scotland, *Nairn
in Darkness and Light*.

After graduating from Oxford he acted as tutor with
an Anglo-Irish family in Co. Roscommon, then for
twenty-six years worked as writer and producer of radio
documentaries at the BBC.

The People of the Sea is an account of the men and
women he met and the tales they told as he walked
the countryside of Ireland and the Isles in search of
seal-lore, and demonstrates the powerful poetic charge
carried by straight and modest narration.

'What made you stop sealing?' I asked him, after a while.

'It was my father's trade, but he died, as I was telling you,
soon after my mother, before I was twenty years of age—and
I had to mind the house and bit of land here for the brothers
and sisters. And at that time, too, there was this landlord I
was telling you about—a man most constantly set against
the killing of the seals.'

'Yes. Yes,' said Tadhg, as though he didn't want to hear
any more.

'Well, several parties came over to the house from time
to time looking for a drop of seal oil. It was a great cure,
you know, Tadhg, and is yet, for all kinds of sprains and
rheumatism and one thing and another like that. And the
people here used to get it from my father, so they did
expect the same from me after his death. And I didn't like
to disappoint them—although to tell the truth I had enough
and more to do at home without that part of my father's
business on the top of it. However, they'd be sending word,
and sending word for seal oil, and some of them walking
down from the mountains only to find me without a drop for

98

them. So I made up my mind to get a seal and satisfy them. So out with me one morning with the gun, for I thought I'd best get one in the daylight on the strand below the cliff. I thought to myself, you know, that it would be easier on myself to get one that way, rather than go into the cave with the boat and get one there—myself single-handed with the boat and a dead seal in the darkness of the cave. So out with me then, and who did I meet but the landlord himself.

' "Good morning," says he.

' "Good morning, sir," says I. " 'Tis a grand sunny day," says I. "I thought to get a rabbit," says I, "on a sunny day like this—something for to give the children to their dinner."

' "I see," says the landlord, and he looks at me. "Well, Sean," says he, "I see the world is upside down."

' "There's no harm, I hope, sir," says I, "if I go and get a rabbit for the children to their dinner."

' "There's no harm in that, Sean," says he, "but there's harm in it surely," says he, "when the rabbits leave the hill and go down to the edge of the water," says he. "They'll likely next be feeding off the seaweed," says he, "and you making your way over the sands at low tide for to shoot them."

' "I thought to get one on the top of the cliff," says I. "I saw a dozen of them feeding there last evening."

' "And tell me this," says the landlord to me: "Did you ever see them feeding there at noon on a hot summer's day?"

' "I did not, sir!"

' "And what time is it now?"

' "About noon, sir."

' "About noon on a hot summer's day."

'That was the last he said to me. And from that I knew well that he knew I was after the seals. So I just took a little walk for myself by the edge o' the cliff. And I saw two big seals lying there below on the strand. But I left them where they lay and went home. I thought it all out in the night, how I could get this seal, and the only time, God forgive me, that I knew I was safe from the landlord was on a Sunday morning when he would be at Mass. So I planned all well for that time. I took my gun out by night, on the Saturday night, and I hid it underneath the clump of furze bushes that was growing by the cliff. And on the Sunday morning I put on my suit the same as usual as though to go to Mass. And I walked out away from the chapel up the road towards the point where I thought to myself I'd meet no one, mine being the last house out, the same as you see it to-day. And I walked on and the day was bright. And who did I meet but the landlord again himself.

' "Good morning," says he. "So you're walking away from Mass this morning," he says.

' "Good morning, sir," says I, and the funny thing was I was thinking nearly the same way about him as he was thinking about me—wondering to myself how he was so far off from his own right road to Mass. But I thought to myself "it is well I'm not carrying the gun", and I wasn't so much afraid as the first time.

'So I told him I had a cousin married in the next parish, and that I had it in mind to go and see her that day. And I said if I took the cliff road and cut across the bog beyond I would reach that other chapel well in time for second Mass and see my cousin after.

' "Well, Sean," says he, "you're a good man and I hope your cousin's grateful when she sees the long road you took to see her."

' "I'll think I'll find it quicker than the other road," says I.

' "The quickest road is the road your mind is set on." says he, and he went on to Mass.

'When I knew it was safe I slipped down the path between the cliffs to the strand. There's a big rock there, and coming up quietly, I lay behind it to use it as a hide. I saw five seals lying there, four cows and a bull. The bull lay nearest to me and he was a big one, but I saw nothing at the time to remark in the way his coat was spotted. I shot him fair and he was dead before the others reached the water's edge. Well, I had a long job before me then, and a small space of time for it, to get it done before Mass would be over. I had to go for the horse and the ropes and make him fast and haul him up the path of the cliff and along the road to the house here.

'Well, I left the skinning until after nightfall, and I never saw the landlord more for a week. But when I was skinning this seal I did take notice of a white mark he had on him by the side of his neck, a strange shape of a mark, like three links of a chain. There was not more than six inches in the whole of it, and you never would remark it unless you looked close. So anyways I thought nothing about it, only to look at it once. And I hung the skin behind the house here, and I got the big stones and the pans that hadn't been used since my father fell sick of the fever, and I put the blubber between them to press the oil out. And some of the meat I brought into the house and cooked it for the children. Did you ever taste the meat of the seal?'

'I did not,' said Tadhg, 'but I once smelt it.'

'I was sore afraid of the smell in case maybe the landlord would pass and find me out. But it wasn't that way he found me. It wasn't until the week was over that I met him again, and this time it was after Mass at our own chapel. He rode his horse beside me a piece of the way home.

' "Sean," says he, "I have lost one of my seals." That's what he said to me.

' "I beg your pardon, sir," says I.

' "I think it's one of the bulls," says the landlord, "and I'm beginning to think he's come to some harm."

' "I understand, sir," says I.

' "It's a week since I saw him," says the landlord, looking at me very straight. "As a matter of fact it was on a Sunday on the way to Mass, just before meeting you, I saw this seal."

'I took a bit of courage then, and "I'm not sure but you might be mistaken, sir," says I, "for no man can count the seals in the sea."

' "You think not," says the landlord.

' "It would be a hard job surely."

' "Every one of them is different," says the landlord. "I would know them apart as well as you would know your own brothers and sisters one from another. And I know when one of them is missing as well as you would know if your brother was missing."

'I said nothing to that.

' "Well you don't believe me, Sean," says the landlord.

' "I do believe you surely," says I, "but the sea is big

and the seal cave itself is dark, with great numbers of seals lying in it."

' "Well now," says the landlord to me, "you would know your own cattle and your sheep, would you not?"

' "I would."

' "No matter if you had a hundred or two hundred of them—and you'd be able to go in among them at night and pick out those you wanted for the fair in the morning."

' "I would, of course, sir. Any man could do that, with his own."

' "Well, Sean," says he, "I know my own seals—them that have their living in the seal cave at the Point beyond—I know them the very same as you would know your beasts."

' "To do that," says I, "you'd nearly need to count them, the same as a man would count his beasts."

' "And I do count them, Sean," says he. "Will you believe me that? And I am very grieved that this old bull is gone—he was one that had a mark on him, Sean. He had a white mark like three links of a chain by the side of his neck."

'What would you do, Tadgh,' said Sean, 'if you found yourself facing a landlord like that?'

'You couldn't well hope to hide what you'd done.'

'You could not. Well, I went home. But I had it so on my mind I couldn't rest. Day nor night I couldn't feel easy, until on the third day I went over to the landlord's house and I told him it was I who shot the seal.'

'And what did he say?' asked Tadhg.

'He said nothing first, only looked at me the same as before. Then I asked him would I bring him the skin, and he shouted at me then. "Go home out of this!" he said.'

'Did you hear more about it?'

'Never a word. He never spoke a word to me from that day. And I never shot another seal since.'

[from *The People of the Sea*, pp. 70–4]

Ghosts

from A CHILDHOOD IN SCOTLAND

The pages below open a fresh and startling memoir, *A Childhood in Scotland*, written by CHRISTIAN MILLER, born in 1920 and brought up in an ancient, ghost-inhabited castle on the vast estate of her tyrannical father.

She became a technical adviser in the Ministry of Production during the Second World War, married in 1942 and has two daughters.

When I was a little girl, the ghosts were more real to me than the people. The people were despotic and changeable, governing my world with a confusing and alarming inconstancy. The ghosts, on the other hand, could be relied on to go about their haunting in a calm and orderly manner. Bearded or bewigged, clad in satin or velvet or nunlike drapery, they whispered their way along the dark corridors of the castle where I was born and spent the first ten years of my life, rarely interfering with or intruding on the lives of the living.

My mother couldn't understand why the servants were frightened of the ghosts. Sitting in the sunny bow window of the Big Drawing Room, she would watch yet another maid—scanty possessions stuffed into a carpet-bag—fleeing down the drive that led through towering beech trees to the main road, and murmur sadly.

'I can never get them to understand that the ghosts won't *hurt* them. If only they'd just ask the poor things what they *want*.' And she would sigh, and bend her head again over her petit point. She was working on a set of covers for the dining-room chairs, a Sisyphean task, for even if she had completed the full set of twenty-four—which she never succeeded in doing—by the time the last was done the first cover would have worn out, and she would have been compelled to start all over again.

Her concentration on her needlework was probably not helped by the fact that she had six ebullient children—known, in pairs, as the Girls, the Boys, and the Children. I was the younger Child, the last of her family. The Boys were sent to school in England when they were about eight, and the Girls when they were thirteen, so during most of my childhood they were home only during the long school holidays—four weeks in the winter, three weeks at Easter, eight weeks in the summer. But we Children—myself and a sister three years older—were, during all our years in the castle, too young to be sent away to school. Whether it was termtime or holidays, we lived in the castle, and it was dinned into us that if we found ourselves face to face with a ghost we must ask it what it wanted. 'They only haunt because they're worried, poor things,' my mother would explain in her soft voice. 'Ask them if there is anything you can *do* for them. And for goodness' sake don't be frightened. After all, they're all your ancestors—whatever is there to be frightened of?'

So, as a child, I was never scared of the ghosts. But I didn't go out of my way to meet them, either. I respected their privacy, and they mine.

There were four chief ghosts in the castle. The quietest was an old man in a velvet coat, who used to sit reading in the library; he was so peaceful that one could be in the room for several minutes without even noticing that he was there, but as soon as one did notice he would softly vanish, fading into the leather upholstery. The woman in a long grey dress was just as untroublesome; her face half covered with a sort of bandage similar to that worn by some orders of nuns, she would come through the wall-cupboard of the nursery and bend over the babies in their cradles, like a nurse checking to see if her charges were sleeping peacefully. Equally unobtrusive was the woman who regularly crossed one of the upper rooms of the tower and vanished into a loft; her only fault was that she did not know that since her time the room had been converted into a bathroom, and her sudden appearance sometimes unnerved male guests who, surprised in the bath, were almost relieved to discover that the woman who had entered was only a spectre. Far from quiet, however, was the red-haired young man on the stairs. He was a ghost who loved parties, and he could be relied on to turn up whenever there was festivity. Ceremonial evening dress for men having changed hardly at all for at least a hundred years, his appearance in kilt, sporran trimmed with ermine-tails, lace-edged shirt and silver-buttoned jacket, excited no particular comment among the merrymakers. It was only when some elderly woman guest would petulantly ask my mother to tell 'the young man with the red beard' not to push past people on the stairs that my mother would know he was out again. But anyone who slept in the tower could hear him on non-party nights as well, laughing and joking with his friends as he ran lightly up and down the steep spiral stairs. Often, after I was promoted from the nursery to a room in the tower, I would lie awake in the dark, with the blankets pulled high under my chin, listening to the ghosts. But I never could make out what it was that they said.

[from *A Childhood in Scotland*, pp. 1–3]

ROBERT MCLELLAN

The Trap

from LINMILL STORIES

ROBERT MCLELLAN (1907–85) dedicated himself to
writing plays in Scots, sixteen for the stage and five
for radio. He lived from 1938 on the Isle of Arran.
The *Linmill Stories* were written for radio and describe
boyhood days on his grandparents' farm near Lanark.
This story begins with the boy watching his grandfather
prepare traps, then helping to set them. He cannot wait
to see if they have caught a rabbit.

Whan I rase in the mornin he was oot and awa, and I was
sair disjaskit, for I had wantit to gang roun and look the
traps. The snaw had gane aff, sae I was alloued oot to play,
though I was telt to be shair and no wade ower the buit heids.
I gaed aboot the closs for a while, though wi aabody awa it
was gey dreich. I gaed into the stable and had a look at the
twa horses that werena oot, syne I gaed into the byre and
watchit the beasts munchin their hey, syne I gaed into the
beyler-hoose. The fires hadna ben lichtit yet, and it was gey
daurk and cauld. In a wee while I had slippit oot o the closs
mou. I couldna keep my mind aff the traps. My grandfaither
had said the day afore that he wad be lookin them first thing
in the mornin, but I thocht that mebbe wi the roads needin
clearin he had forgotten them, and if there were ony rabbits
catchit they wad still be lyin oot.

But could I mind whaur the traps had been set? I gaed to
ae place efter anither, feelin shair that I had been there the
day afore, but ae ash plant was juist like anither, and sae
were the stanes dug up oot o the ditch at the hedge fute,
and it was my grandfaither, and no me, that had meisurt aa
the distances frae yetts; and nae suner had I gane forrit to a
place whaur I was shair there was a trap than I fand I was
wrang, for deil a trap could I fin. They had been ower weill
hidden. But in the end I fand the last trap we had set, ane at

the heid o the tap park at the faur end frae the Lesmahagow road. It was easier to fin nor the ithers, mebbe, because it was lyin juist whaur a hedge atween twa o Tam o Law's parks met the mairch wi Linmill. But it wasna juist that aither. It hadna been hidden weill. There were nae leaves ower the jaws, nor mouls ower the wee airn plate.

I sat on my hunkers weill in by the hedge, thinkin that shairly if there had been a rabbit in ony o the traps I wad hae seen it, and I could haurdly believe that my grandfaither had dune aa his wark for naething. Ae thing was shair, he had haen nae chance o catchin a rabbit in the last trap, it was sae plain to see.

I wonert if I could try to hide it better, but I had seen how cannie my grandfaither was, whan he was coverin them up, and I kent it was a gey kittle maitter. Shairly, though, I could drap a wheen withert leaves ower the jaws withoot pittin my fingers near them. I gaed alang the hedge and gethert some, though they were gey near into mouls wi the winter sae faur on, and ill to fin, but afore lang I had gethert aa I needit, and drappit them ower the trap frae weill abune it. They fell doun on it lichtly, and gey near covert it, but no juist to my likin. Ye could still see ane o the jaws stickin up, and hauf o the wee airn plate. I pat doun my haund and warkit some o the leaves ower the ae jaw that was still showin, and managed to hide it at last. Nou for the airn plate. I had to pit my fingers inside the jaws to win at the mouls on it, but I thocht that if I was licht wi my touch, and juist gied the mouls a wee bit tig and drew my haund awa like lichtnin, I wad be safe eneuch.

I was wrang. I had to lean forrit a wee to rax ower to the trap, and I lost my balance. My haund gaed doun on the airn plate wi aa my wecht abune it. The jaws lowpit up and fastent on fower o my fingers, juist ablow the knuckles. I had been scaudit ance, whan a pan o saut fish had faaen aff the Linmill range, and the pain in my haund was juist like that scaud. And no juist my haund; I could feel it in by breist tae, and in ae side o my neck. It was mair nor I could thole, and I grat oot lood.

I dinna ken hou lang I grat, doun on my knees, leanin on the haund that wasna catchit, and juist wishin I could dee. I cried for my grandfaither, ower and ower again, syne I cried for my grannie, and in the end I was cryin for my minnie, though she was awa in Hamilton wi my daddie.

Nae help cam, and the pain grew waur, and I kent I wad hae to dae something by mysell. I thocht I could mebbe get my fute on the spring and lowse the jaws, but I couldna staun up, and though I managed to get my fute on the spring I could pit nae wecht on it. Then I thocht o tryin to pou the peg oot o the grun, but I had juist ae haund, and it wasna eneuch. I began to see that if naebody cam I wad be there till it grew daurk. I tried to lift the trap aff the grun sae that I could turn roun, but the wecht o the trap made the pain waur, and I had to pit it doun afore I had managed to move.

I tried turnin my heid and lookin ower my shouther, and for a wee while I had a view o the hallie ablow me, wi Linmill lyin in the middle. I could juist see the snaw-covert rufes, and the back waa o the cairt shed. The closs mou was on the side o the steidin, juist oot o sicht, and the hoose was at the faur end, facin the ither wey. It wasna likely that onyane no lookin for me wad come in sicht, and I didna feel I could yell muckle langer. I had to stop lookin, for the twistin o my heid threw me oot o balance, and I could feel my wecht gaun ower on my sair haund. I sat and grat again, and began to woner when they wad miss me. Shairly by tea-time, whan my grandfaither cam back wi the snaw-plew. But I wadna see the plew comin back, wi the closs-mou oot o sicht, sae that was smaa comfort. And whan they did miss me they wadna ken whaur to look, for I hadna said whaur I was gaun. I began to feel shair I wad be oot aa nicht, and wad dee o cauld and stervation, and I gat into a panic and roared like a bull, but naebody heard me, for I gied a pou at the trap and managed to turn hauf roun, and aa I could see was the white snaw and the blank waa o the back of the steidin. My pain gat sae bad wi the pouin at the trap that I had to gie up roarin and juist sit and thole.

I herd a terrible squeal then and lookit alang the hedge, and saw something movin. It was a rabbit, catchit in anither o the traps. I stertit to greit again, into mysell. Then I heard my grandfaither caain my name. He was faurer alang the hedge, comin my wey. I answert him and he saw me, and cam rinnin forrit. In a wee while he had putten his fute on the spring and opent the trap jaws, and I drew my haund oot. When I saw it I gey near fentit. Whaur the teeth o the trap had grippit my fingers they were juist aboot cut in twa. The skin wasna broken, though, but it was crushed richt into the bane, and the teeth marks were blae. The ends o my fingers were like talla. My grandfaither liftit me and pat my heid on his breist and carrit me awa doun hame.

He said no a word aboot me gaun to look the traps. Naither did my grannie, but she yokit on to my grandfaither for lettin me gang wi him whan he set them, and caaed him a sumph and a gommeril and aa that was stippit, till he lost his temper wi her and telt her to shut her gub. I didna want ony tea, and my grannie pat me to my bed. They gaed on flytin at ane anither aa through tea-time, till I wished wi aa my hairt they wad stop.

Then I mindit.

'Grandfaither?'

'Ay, son, what is it?'

'There's a rabbit in a trap, grandfaither. It was squealin.'

'Whaur?'

'Alang the hedge frae whaur ye fand me.'

'Ay, weill, I'll get it in the mornin. Gang to sleep, if ye can.'

'Grandfaither?'

'What is it nou?'

'The rabbit was squealin, grandfaither. I wish ye wad gang and let it oot o the trap.'

'There wad be nae peynt in lettin it gang, son. Its legs'll be hurt.'

My grannie gaed for him.

'Then for guidness' sake awa and pit it oot o its misery. He winna sleep a wink till ye dae.'

My grandfaither rase withoot a word and gaed awa oot again, and I lay and tholed my pain till he came back.

'Did ye kill it, grandfaither?'

'I had to, son. It wad juist hae deeit gin I had let it gang.'

I lay and grat for a while, into mysell, and my grannie and grandfaither sat in their chairs by the fire, as still as daith, no sayin a word.

I maun hae drappit aff to sleep in the end, and in the mornin I could haurdly feel my sair haund, though the marks were still there, and bade there for weeks; and I neir heard as muckle as a mention o rabbits for the rest o that holiday.

[from *Linmill Stories*, pp. 66–70]

SORLEY MACLEAN

Hallaig
from HALLAIG

SORLEY MACLEAN (SOMHAIRLE MACGILL-EAIN) was
born in 1911 on the island of Raasay into a family musical
on both sides. He was educated at Portree High School
and Edinburgh University, became a teacher himself and
was for many years headmaster at Plockton in Wester
Ross. He was wounded while serving in North Africa
during the Second World War and his experiences
produced poems distinguished for their bitter, ironic
compassion.

MacLean's poetry has not only been instrumental in
restoring literary Gaelic in Scotland, it has a force,
strangeness, and nobility peculiarly his own.

HALLAIG

'Time, the deer is in the Wood of Hallaig.'

The window is nailed and boarded
through which I saw the West
and my love is at the Burn of Hallaig
a birch tree, and she has always been

between Inver and Milk Hollow,
here and there about Baile-chuirn:
she is a birch, a hazel,
a straight slender young rowan.

In Screapadal of my people,
where Norman and Big Hector were,
their daughters and their sons are a wood
going up beside the stream.

Proud tonight the pine cocks
crowing on the top of Cnoc an Ra
straight their backs in the moonlight—
they are not the wood I love.

I will wait for the birch wood
until it comes up by the Cairn,
until the whole ridge from Beinn na Lice
will be under its shade.

If it does not, I will go down to Hallaig,
to the sabbath of the dead,
where the people are frequenting,
every single generation gone.

They are still in Hallaig,
Macleans and MacLeods,
all who were there in the time of MacGille Chaluim:
the dead have been seen alive—

HALLAIG

'Tha tim, am fiadh, an Coille Hallaig.'

Tha bùird is tàirnean air an uinneig
triomh 'm faca mi an Aird an Iar
's tha mo ghaol aig Allt Hallaig
'na craoibh bheithe, 's bha i riamh

eadar an t-Inbhir 's Poll a' Bhainne,
thall 's a bhos mu Bhaile-Chùirn:
tha i 'na beithe, 'na calltuinn,
'na caorunn dhìreach sheang ùir.

Ann an Screapadal mo chinnidh,
far robh Tarmad 's Eachunn Mór,
tha 'n nigheanan 's am mic 'nan coille
ag gabhail suas ri taobh an lóin.

Uaibhreach a nochd na coilich ghiuthais
ag gairm air mullach Cnoc an Rà,
dìreach an druim ris a' ghealaich —
chan iadsan coille mo ghràidh.

Fuirichidh mi ris a' bheithe
gus an tig i mach an Càrn,
gus am bi am bearradh uile
o Bheinn na Lice f' a sgàil.

Mura tig 's ann theàrnas mi a Hallaig
a dh' ionnsaigh sàbaid nam marbh,
far a bheil an sluagh a' tathaich,
gach aon ghinealach a dh' fhalbh.

Tha iad fhathast ann a Hallaig,
Clann Ghill-Eain 's Clann MhicLeoid,
na bh' ann ri linn Mhic Ghille-Chaluim:
chunnacas na mairbh beò —

the men lying on the green
at the end of every house that was,
the girls a wood of birches,
straight their backs, bent their heads.

Between the Leac and Fearns
the road is under wild moss
and the girls in silent bands
go to Clachan as in the beginning.

And return from Clachan,
from Suisnish and the land of the living;
each one young and light-stepping,
without the heartbreak of the tale.

From the Burn of Fearns to the raised beach
that is clear in the mystery of the hills,
there is only the congregation of the girls
keeping up the endless walk,

coming back to Hallaig in the evening,
in the dumb living twilight,
filling the steep slopes,
their laughter in my ears a mist,

and their beauty a film on my heart
before the dimness comes on the kyles,
and when the sun goes down behind Dun Cana
a vehement bullet will come from the gun of Love;

and will strike the deer that goes dizzily,
sniffing at the grass-grown ruined homes;
his eye will freeze in the wood;
his blood will not be traced while I live.

na fir 'nan laighe air an lianaig
aig ceann gach taighe a bh' ann,
na h-igheanan 'nan coille bheithe,
dìreach an druim, crom an ceann.

Eadar an Leac is na Feàrnaibh
tha 'n rathad mór fo chòinnich chiùin,
's na h-igheanan 'nam badan sàmhach
a' dol a Chlachan mar o thùs.

Agus a' tilleadh as a' Chlachan,
á Suidhisnis 's á tir nam beò;
a chuile té òg uallach
gun bhristeadh cridhe an sgeòil.

O Allt na Feàrnaibh gus an fhaolinn
tha soilleir an dìomhaireachd nam beann
chan eil ach coimhthional nan nighean
ag cumail na coiseachd gun cheann,

a' tilleadh a Hallaig anns an fheasgar,
anns a' chamhanaich bhalbh bheò,
a' lìonadh nan leathadan casa,
an gàireachdaich 'nam chluais 'na ceò,

's am bòidhche 'na sgleò air mo chridhe
mun tig an ciaradh air na caoil,
's nuair theàrnas grian air cùl Dhùn Cana
thig peileir dian á gunna Ghaoil;

's buailear am fiadh a tha 'na thuaineal
a' snòtach nan làraichean feòir;
thig reothadh air a shùil 'sa choille;
chan fhaighear lorg air fhuil ri m' bheò.

[from *Nua Bhardachd Ghaidhlig*, Modern Scottish Gaelic Poems, pp. 84–8]

CANONGATE CLASSICS

Books listed in alphabetical order by author.

The Bruce John Barbour, edited by AAM Duncan
   ISBN 0 86241 681 7   £9.99 $14.95
The Land of the Leal James Barke
   ISBN 0 86241 142 4   £7.99 $13.99
The House with the Green Shutters
   George Douglas Brown
   ISBN 0 86241 549 7   £4.99 $9.95
The Watcher by the Threshold Shorter Scottish Fiction
   John Buchan
   ISBN 0 86241 682 5   £7.99 $14.95
Witchwood John Buchan
   ISBN 0 86241 202 1   £4.99 $9.95
Lying Awake Catherine Carswell
   ISBN 0 86241 683 3   £5.99 $12.95
Open the Door! Catherine Carswell
   ISBN 0 86241 644 2   £5.99 $12.95
The Life of Robert Burns Catherine Carswell
   ISBN 0 86241 292 7   £5.99 $12.95
Two Worlds David Daiches
   ISBN 0 86241 148 3   £5.99 $12.95
The Complete Brigadier Gerard Arthur Conan Doyle
   ISBN 0 86241 534 9   £5.99 $13.95
Mr Alfred M.A. George Friel
   ISBN 0 86241 163 7   £4.99 $11.95
Dance of the Apprentices Edward Gaitens
   ISBN 0 86241 297 8   £5.99 $11.95
Ringan Gilhaize John Galt
   ISBN 0 86241 552 7   £6.99 $13.95
The Member and *The Radical* John Galt
   ISBN 0 86241 642 6   £5.99 $12.95
A Scots Quair: (Sunset Song, Cloud Howe, Grey
   Granite) Lewis Grassic Gibbon
   ISBN 0 86241 532 2   £5.99 $13.95
Sunset Song Lewis Grassic Gibbon
   ISBN 0 86241 179 3   £4.99 $9.95
Memoirs of a Highland Lady vols. I&II
   Elizabeth Grant of Rothiemurchus
   ISBN 0 86241 396 6   £7.99 $15.95
The Highland Lady in Ireland
   Elizabeth Grant of Rothiemurchus
   ISBN 0 86241 361 3   £7.99 $14.95

Highland River Neil M. Gunn
  ISBN 0 86241 358 3 £5.99 $11.95
Sun Circle Neil M. Gunn
  ISBN 0 86241 587 X £5.99 $11.95
The Well at the World's End Neil M. Gunn
  ISBN 0 86241 645 0 £5.99 $12.95
Gillespie J. MacDougall Hay
  ISBN 0 86241 427 X £6.99 $13.95
The Private Memoirs and Confessions of a Justified Sinner
  James Hogg
  ISBN 0 86241 340 0 £3.99 $8.95
The Three Perils of Man James Hogg
  ISBN 0 86241 646 9 £8.99 $14.95
Fergus Lamont Robin Jenkins
  ISBN 0 86241 310 9 £6.99 $12.95
Just Duffy Robin Jenkins
  ISBN 0 86241 551 9 £4.99 $9.95
The Changeling Robin Jenkins
  ISBN 0 86241 228 5 £4.99 $9.95
Journey to the Hebrides (A Journey to the Western Isles
  of Scotland, The Journal of a Tour to the Hebrides)
  Samuel Johnson & James Boswell
  ISBN 0 86241 588 8 £5.99 $12.95
Tunes of Glory James Kennaway
  ISBN 0 86241 223 4 £3.50 $8.95
A Voyage to Arcturus David Lindsay
  ISBN 0 86241 377 X £4.99 $9.95
Ane Satyre of the Thrie Estaitis Sir David Lindsay
  ISBN 0 86241 191 2 £4.99 $9.95
Magnus Merriman Eric Linklater
  ISBN 0 86241 313 3 £4.95 $9.95
Private Angelo Eric Linklater
  ISBN 0 86241 376 1 £5.95 $11.95
Scottish Ballads Edited by Emily Lyle
  ISBN 0 86241 477 6 £4.99 $13.95
Nua-Bhardachd Ghaidhlig/Modern Scottish Gaelic Poems
  Edited by Donald MacAulay
  ISBN 0 86241 494 6 £4.99 $12.95
The Early Life of James McBey James McBey
  ISBN 0 86241 445 8 £5.99 $11.95
And the Cock Crew Fionn MacColla
  ISBN 0 86241 536 5 £4.99 $11.95
The Devil and the Giro: Two Centuries of Scottish Stories
  Edited by Carl MacDougall
  ISBN 0 86241 359 1 £8.99 $14.95

St Kilda: Island on the Edge of the World Charles Maclean
  ISBN 0 86241 388 5   £5.99 $11.95
Linmill Stories Robert McLellan
  ISBN 0 86241 282 X   £4.99 $11.95
Wild Harbour Ian Macpherson
  ISBN 0 86241 234 X   £3.95 $9.95
A Childhood in Scotland Christian Miller
  ISBN 0 86241 230 7   £4.99 $8.95
The Blood of the Martyrs Naomi Mitchison
  ISBN 0 86241 192 0   £4.95 $11.95
The Corn King and the Spring Queen Naomi Mitchison
  ISBN 0 86241 287 0   £6.95 $12.95
The Gowk Storm Nancy Brysson Morrison
  ISBN 0 86241 222 6   £3.95 $9.95
An Autobiography Edwin Muir
  ISBN 0 86241 423 7   £5.99 $11.95
The Wilderness Journeys (The Story of My Boyhood and
  Youth, A Thousand Mile Walk to the Gulf, My First
  Summer in the Sierra, Travels in Alaska, Stickeen)
  John Muir
  ISBN 0 86241 586 1   £8.99 $14.95
Imagined Selves: (Imagined Corners, Mrs Ritchie,
  Mrs Grundy in Scotland, Women: An Inquiry, Women
  in Scotland) Willa Muir
  ISBN 0 86241 605 1   £8.99 $14.95
Homeward Journey John MacNair Reid
  ISBN 0 86241 178 5   £3.95 $9.95
A Twelvemonth and a Day Christopher Rush
  ISBN 0 86241 439 3   £4.99 $11.95
End of an Old Song J. D. Scott
  ISBN 0 86241 311 7   £4.95 $11.95
Grampian Quartet: (The Quarry Wood, The
  Weatherhouse, A Pass in the Grampians, The Living
  Mountain) Nan Shepherd
  ISBN 0 86241 589 6   £8.99 $14.95
Consider the Lilies Iain Crichton Smith
  ISBN 0 86241 415 6   £4.99 $11.95
Listen to the Voice: Selected Stories Iain Crichton Smith
  ISBN 0 86241 434 2   £5.99 $11.95
Diaries of a Dying Man William Soutar
  ISBN 0 86241 347 8   £4.99 $11.95
Shorter Scottish Fiction Robert Louis Stevenson
  ISBN 0 86241 555 1   £4.99 $13.95

Tales of Adventure (Black Arrow, Treasure Island, 'The
   Sire de Malétroit's Door' and other stories) Robert
   Louis Stevenson
   ISBN 0 86241 687 6   £7.99 $14.95
Tales of the South Seas (Island Landfalls, The Ebb-tide,
   The Wrecker) Robert Louis Stevenson
   ISBN 0 86241 643 4   £7.99 $14.95
The Scottish Novels: (Kidnapped, Catriona, The Master
   of Ballantrae, Weir of Hermiston) Robert Louis
   Stevenson
   ISBN 0 86241 533 0   £5.99 $13.95
The People of the Sea David Thomson
   ISBN 0 86241 550 0   £4.99 $11.95
City of Dreadful Night James Thomson
   ISBN 0 86241 449 0   £4.99 $11.95
Three Scottish Poets: MacCaig, Morgan, Lochead
   ISBN 0 86241 400 8   £4.99 $11.95
Black Lamb and Grey Falcon Rebecca West
   ISBN 0 86241 428 8   £10.99

ORDERING INFORMATION

Most Canongate Classics are available at good bookshops.
You can also order direct from Canongate Books Ltd – by
post: 14 High Street, Edinburgh EH1 1TE, or by telephone:
0131 557 5111. There is no charge for postage and packing to
customers in the United Kingdom.

Canongate Classics are distributed exclusively in the
USA and Canada by:

Interlink Publishing Group, Inc.
46 Crosby Street
Northampton, MA 01060–1804
Tel: (413) 582–7054
Fax: (413) 582–7057
e-mail: interpg@aol.com